(

JUDITH VON HALLE, born in Berlin in 1972, attended school in Germany and the USA and subsequently studied architecture, graduating in 1998. She first encountered anthroposophy in 1997, and began working as a member of staff at Rudolf Steiner House in Berlin, where she also lectured from 2001. In addition she had her own architectural practice. In 2004 she received the stigmata, which transformed her life. Her first book was published in German in 2005, and she now works principally as a lecturer and author. She lives in Berlin with her husband.

By the same author:

SECRETS OF THE STATIONS OF THE CROSS AND THE GRAIL BLOOD

The Mystery of Transformation

Judith von Halle

TEMPLE LODGE

Translated by Matthew Barton

Temple Lodge Publishing
Hillside House, The Square
Forest Row, RH18 5ES

www.templelodge.com

Published by Temple Lodge 2007

Originally published in German under the title *Von den Geheimnissen des Kreuzweges und des Gralsblutes* by Verlag am Goetheanum, Dornach, 2006

A catalogue record for this book is available from the British Library

ISBN 978 1 902636 89 4

Cover by Andrew Morgan Design featuring 'The Crucifixion', detail from the 'Bernwardstür', Hildesheim Cathedral (*c.* 1015)
Typeset by DP Photosetting, Neath, West Glamorgan
Printed and bound by Cromwell Press Limited, Trowbridge, Wiltshire

Approaches to Understanding the Christ Event

Volume 2

Foreword

This foreword aims to give some answers to questions I am repeatedly asked when I give lectures, or take part in discussion seminars.*

An unprepared reader might, quite understandably, be taken aback by the mode and content of some passages in this volume, since it includes descriptions of historical and supersensible facts and events which are related as self-evident truths without any reference to substantiating sources.

In actual personal encounter one can gain an authentic impression of the speaker, but in the inevitable absence of open-hearted personal contact with my reader — which makes it far easier to create a mood of human trust and dialogue as the basis for

---

* While these questions have already been dealt with in the Introduction to the collection of lectures by Judith von Halle published under the title *And If He Has Not Been Raised..., The Stations of Christ's Path to Spirit Man* (Temple Lodge Publishing 2007) not every reader will be familiar with this book. (Editor's note.)

clear communication – I will try to record what I have to say in writing. I have formulated the following explanations and answers very precisely, knowing that such clarity could be interpreted as lack of modesty. At the same time though – which is why I am willing to take this risk – such clarity alone makes it possible to give anything like a full answer to questions that people ask me.

The contents of this volume have arisen from my own spiritual experience, and do not represent any kind of hypothesis or speculation, except where I expressly say that I am unable to make any definitive statement about a particular event or set of circumstances.

However, not every description stems from the same source of experience and perception. My spiritual experience relates, on the one hand, to a direct – one could even say sensory – involvement in the historical events at the time of Christ. This experience, granted to me following a process beginning in 2004 in which I received the stigmata, can be pictured as a kind of 'travelling back in time', involving all the sensory impressions we can have during ordinary waking life, but now in relation to a particular epoch and location. Thus the experience is not based on so-called visions or pure clairvoyance, nor imaginative pictures, but rather on direct witnessing of what actually happened on earth. Besides visual perceptions of the individuals participating in the events at the time of Christ, together with their surroundings, culture and way of life, all other senses available to us in normal waking consciousness are also involved. For instance the language being spoken can be heard, the ground beneath one's feet is felt, as are cold or heat.

The other source for the content presented here is quite different, yet no less authentic. It will be clear where accounts of the historical events pass over into a spiritual-scientific mode of observation.* This may well appear more neutral and sober than descriptions of sensory experience at the time of

_____

* The term spiritual science refers to an investigation of spiritual realities which applies objective rigour of the kind only otherwise found in modern science. The word 'anthroposophy', often referred to in this volume, literally means 'wisdom of the human being' and is a body of knowledge acquired through spiritual science. (Editor's note.)

Christ. This is no doubt right and proper from a certain perspective, since it involves as precise a 'translation' as possible of what is present and perceptible in the world of spirit. We can access intuitions of these cosmic facts when our ego or 'I', on passing beyond the threshold, separates entirely from the astral sphere so that we — or in other words our 'I' — enter the realm of objectivity. Everyone has impressions of this kind during sleep, yet we rarely succeed in carrying these back into waking consciousness. It is a difficult task, and therefore one which involves great responsibility, to transform these objective facts which our 'I' has absorbed beyond the threshold into real knowledge that is as truthful as is ordinary sense perception on its own, self-apparent, terms. We need to check repeatedly whether our spiritual perception truly corresponds to the conceptual framework to which we assign it. Only when all results stand up in the face of such scrutiny should the pupil of spiritual science feel entitled to pass on his findings as spiritual knowledge.

Many people have spiritual perceptions nowadays

(one often hears that this faculty is on the increase) — for instance on the etheric or astral plane.* These perceptions remain useless however, or can often even trigger grave confusion, if their real nature and context remains hidden to those who have them. For instance, someone may have perceptions of the etheric world, immersing himself in the sphere of elemental nature beings.† Yet statements about the elemental kingdom can only stand up to scrutiny, can only be truly objective, when we resurface again from that plane: in other words, when we do not solely immerse ourselves in the elemental beings'

---

* In Steiner's view, and that of the author, we possess, apart from our mineralized physical body, an etheric or life body which we share with the plant kingdom, and an astral or soul body which we have in common with animals. The etheric body is chiefly associated with rhythms, circulation and habitual ways of doing things, while the astral body is the seat of passions, emotions and soul. The fourth, and eternal aspect of our being, is the 'I' or ego which continues to exist after death and subsequently seeks reincarnation in a new body. (Editor's note.)
† Elemental beings are living but non-physical entities that exist in the various kingdoms of nature, of which human beings used to have more awareness. We find reference to them in folk-tales and literature as nature spirits (such as fire and water spirits). (Editor's note.)

plane of experience but as it were raise it one level higher: to a perspective and point of observation from which we can not only report on the nature of the elemental word, but can also have knowledge *about* this world. It is like swimming in a great expanse of water, an experience which enables us to say that the water is deep and cold. But only when we emerge into the air again like a bird can we judge whether this stretch of water is actually a large lake or possibly an ocean, and whether and where the water is surrounded by land or not, and which continent it is on. So before we can authentically integrate our perceptions into a wider, overall context, they always need to be examined from a higher standpoint.

It is spiritual science's achievement that we are nowadays able to transform our perceptions through clear, trained thinking, into knowledge that is faithful to truth and reality.

The statements in this volume which do not contain sensory-based perceptions of events at the time of Christ derive from the source of knowledge just referred to. They are expressed cautiously, and with an appropriate sense of earnestness, and are in no way speculative interpretations. For this reason they may strike the reader as more factual or impersonal than the other accounts. This is due to the above-mentioned supra-personal level of objectivity beyond the threshold. Despite this they are my own authentic spiritual findings; and where, in contrast, they represent the findings of Rudolf Steiner, this is expressly stated.

This second type of spiritual perception is not in any way a consequence of stigmatization, since it was present before this occurred. Since then, though, it has intensified.

After my lectures were published in book form, some people asked me to give a precise exposition of my supposed path of schooling. I fully understand what underlies this desire, but apart from the fact that it was not my aim to address such issues in this book — since I do not wish to make my own destiny the main subject of my deliberations, but instead to use the resources available to render the Christ event more comprehensible — such a 'development manual' would be very short and probably not at all of the kind that people wish or imagine. The mode of perception described above was already present in my early years, doubtless as a consequence of previous lives, and did not necessitate me pursuing, in this life, the arduous path of a hermit with all kinds of mortifications of the flesh and renunciations before my spiritual eyes were opened. Nor did it exclude, however, a certain discipline in my life as consequence of self-evident engagement with spiritual realities. My discipline or spiritual reverence in this life can be seen as a consequence of preparation. Nevertheless, 'continuity of awareness' beyond the threshold is always only possible when, with the greatest engagement and commitment, one has absorbed and continues to absorb the Christ event; when, in a way that is devoted, loving, humble and grateful, one turns not only one's heart and soul but also one's powers of enquiry to the world of spirit — until one feels so strongly moved by that greatest of all events in humanity's evolution that one starts to feel a tangible sense of the stigmata. Then one can have the profound experience that the great sacrifice of the Redeemer was also accomplished for each one of us, for our own humble being — within which, however, lies the seed of the divine.

Thus my potential to live consciously into the spiritual cosmos — also described as continuity of awareness — was already present before stigmatization occurred. When I also started experiencing the historical events at first hand, rather than this remaining pure experience I was able to bring together my capacity for supersensible knowledge with the historical events I witnessed. You could say that the tool was already present before the material it was to work upon. If you want to construct a violin you need a reliable tool ready to hand before you begin — rather than starting to make one at the same time as the instrument you're making. Without a tool you may have the finest wood as raw material, but you will be unable to make a violin with it. In the present case, supersensible power of knowledge can provide the necessary tool for investigating the spiritual background to sensory processes and historical events.

Berlin, March 2006   *Judith von Halle*

Introduction

People repeatedly ask about the etheric Christ — how one can find Him and whether it might not be more important to devote oneself to the etheric sphere in which the Christ being can appear to human beings in the present and the future, rather than to events at the turning point of time. This question is justified, for the appearance of Christ in the etheric world is an event made possible by the end of Kali Yuga* (1899) and therefore something now accessible to direct experience. Perception of the etheric Christ takes place at a period of human evolution in which we have developed a high degree of individuality, and awareness of our individuality. Experiences relating to perception of the being of Christ are correspondingly individual. There is no single schema or set of required conditions dictating

---

* The Dark Age, during which the human being entered ever deeper into matter, and the worlds of spirit were more hidden from him. (Editor's note.)

how such an encounter occurs. Both the spiritual content of the experiences connected with it and perception of His manifestation are always individual – as is the utterly distinctive personality of each human being. It is a signature of the essence of Christ that He reveals Himself to the individual ego or 'I' in the way that can only, uniquely, occur for this particular soul.

It is because these experiences are so individual that I believe they should, initially, be nurtured in quiet, inner life rather than passing immediately into a public forum, especially as an encounter with the Christ-being unquestionably belongs to the most intimate, and often life-changing spiritual experiences we can have today. Experience has shown that such an encounter can become the source of ethical actions in daily life. It can lead to an unwavering trust in spiritual guidance, and to forthright courage in standing up for spiritual realities in today's world. Thus, without ever coming to public discussion, an encounter with the etheric Christ is usually a force of impetus, invisible to the external world, for free, responsible actions by an individual human being, fulfilling a lofty task in personal 'I' development.

People can and may share their experiences, of course; but today there is a widespread tendency towards a certain spiritual sensationalism that asks, for instance, what the etheric Christ looks like. Or even a prevalent view that one is only a spiritual individual worthy of serious attention if one has had an encounter with this being. Attitudes such as these which are, however, only rarely admitted, make it enormously difficult to give this theme the serious attention it certainly requires.

Encounters with the Christ, which often occur spontaneously, are experienced by individual people, also in non-anthroposophical settings. Even allowing for the silence of many such people about these experiences, we can nevertheless say that so far no 'mass' perception of the manifestation of Christ has occurred.

There are a whole range of reasons for this, certainly, which I do not intend to pursue here. But the question remains: How can we find the Christ-being in the etheric world? What possibilities are there for those who have not yet had any conscious experience of the etheric Christ to penetrate to perception of His being?

Anthroposophical spiritual science aims to prepare humanity for perceiving the etheric Christ. Each individual can advance on the path of spiritual-scientific knowledge through practical exercises and inner schooling, so that — even without direct experience in the realm we are discussing — he can gain his own unique, immediate access to knowledge of the Son of God.

But once someone has decided to inwardly cultivate anthroposophy in himself, as the right means of attaining spiritual awareness appropriate for our times, he directly engages his will in developing knowledge of the Mystery of Golgotha; for alongside the personal and suprapersonal impetus of the individuality of Rudolf Steiner, anthroposophy owes its fundamental direction solely to the Christ event. Thus anthroposophy leads us directly to the knowledge that spiritual-scientific reflection on the Christ mystery is, at the same time, a preoccupation with true insight into the

nature of the human being, with his inner and
outer nature, in a way that is fully appropriate to
contemporary needs. When we strive to plumb the
essence of the universal representative of humanity, we also plumb our own depths through Him.
We gain insight into our own humanity, encountering both our sensory and supersensory nature,
when we turn our attention to the Mystery of Golgotha as illumined by anthroposophical spiritual
science.

If we repeatedly take this step on the path of
schooling; if, through devoting ourselves to
Christ's sacrifice for humanity, knowledge of our
own nature begins to ripen, then we create the
foundation for seeing into higher worlds, and thus
for perceiving the Christ being in the etheric
world.

To gaze daily on the Mystery of Golgotha with
thirsting soul and spirit is neither an outmoded nor
antiquated spiritual practice. On the contrary, the
Mystery of Golgotha awaits full understanding
through the forces of consciousness of today's
spiritually striving human beings, giving them the

potential for higher existence conferred on 'your own I / For its free will'.*

If we take the first step – devotion to the Mystery of Golgotha in the search for knowledge and insight – *before* the second, we can safely and certainly attain our goal. And even if we have already taken the second or third step, we will find our way back to the point of departure and recognize that subsequent steps do not diminish its significance. We will then increasingly learn to value and revere its majesty, beauty and complexity; for the starting point contains all possible future steps within it, which cannot be taken without this originating source. The further the true pupil of the spirit advances in initiation, the more deeply he bows down before this original spring of all existence and of his own striving and search. A master who ultimately succeeds in penetrating the furthest reaches of the world of spirit will only then come finally to true insight into the source of evolution. This source of revelation of the mysteries of humanity is the incarnation of God on earth.

---

* From Rudolf Steiner's Foundation Stone Meditation. See *The Foundation Stone Meditation* (Rudolf Steiner Press 2005).

To perceive Christ in the etheric is a further step on the path of knowledge of the mysteries of humanity, for then the human being begins to see the Redeemer in a new form of manifestation. Thus our understanding of Christ is transformed through the ages, and it is the task of each succeeding generation to develop further the image of Christ step by step, adapting it to the actual content of the mysteries. We need to engage in this demanding work to develop a contemporary understanding of Christ. And even someone who has already been granted a perception of the etheric Christ can turn again, with new eyes, with newly awoken thirst of will, to the Mystery of Golgotha, the event from which all human evolution takes its source.

The efforts to develop deeper understanding of Christ in this volume should be seen in this light.

Berlin, August 2006   *Judith von Halle*

I

THE MYSTERY OF GOLGOTHA AND FORMATION OF THE RESURRECTION BODY

The following commentary draws on a spiritual-scientific perspective to explore two stages of the Mystery of Golgotha which at first glance do not seem to be directly connected. But in their deeper background they should not be regarded as in any way separate, even if the spear wound — in purely chronological terms — does not follow directly on from the Stations of the Cross. In the course of this account it will become clear to what extent reflection on one aspect can enhance understanding of the other. If we turn our focus to the Christ event, drawing on anthroposophical methods to do so, we will find that the purely temporal context of historical events recedes increasingly into the background as, in a great panorama, insight into its spiritual interconnections increasingly dawns on us.

If we wish to approach the mystery of the spear

wound we can do so from many different angles; and I want to stress that the following explorations do not claim to be the whole picture. It is a fact — and remains so — that the great, universal event which we also call the Mystery of Golgotha is immeasurable in its significance for the human spirit in our time, and thus an inexhaustible source of revelation for every person who embarks on the spiritual-scientific path of knowledge. The most diverse intuitions can arise for each seeker. Inasmuch as these are true intuitions they will never contradict one another but, however varied they seem, merely illumine the same event from different viewpoints.

When we begin to observe events at the turning point of time more closely, we can feel how our inner life longingly turns to something to which we so decisively owe our inner freedom and capacity to develop. In our soul there spreads a reverent, elevated mood indispensable for inner work and devotion to the Mystery of Golgotha — both for consideration of the historical events and for spiritual-scientific work. When, to gain understanding of the special significance of Jesus Christ's wounds, it becomes necessary to fully include the profound and comprehensive wealth of knowledge contained in Rudolf Steiner's spiritual science; when we no longer merely pursue accounts of the historical events but work our way into the most demanding realms of spiritual-scientific knowledge of the human being, then also, and in particular, we need to draw on this festive and elevated mood.

If we want to turn our attention to the spear wound we must first pursue a series of prior explorations to render its deeper meaning comprehensible. It will help us to grasp the spear wound mystery if we first differentiate it from the other wounds that were inflicted on Christ Jesus.

The figure of the resurrected Christ on Easter morning shows both the spear wound and the four marks of crucifixion. On the famous Isenheim Altar not only are the four wounds correctly positioned but Matthias Grünewald has also masterfully translated the stance and gestures of Christ's resurrected corporeality into the language of painting. Above and beyond this, however, Grünewald has, in his depiction of the Crucifixion scene on the back of the altar, also drawn attention to a particular circumstance. There, in marked contrast to the resurrection figure, the terribly ravaged and violated body of the Lord is portrayed.

The Gospels only hint at the torments which the Redeemer had to undergo before he was nailed to the Cross.

Yet we may ask why the depiction of the resurrection body shows the wounds of the Crucifixion but not the appalling marks of torture caused by His flagellation and His falling while bearing the Cross.

Evolution of the archetypal spiritual-physical human form

In addressing this question we should not assume — as repeatedly suggested nowadays — that the *material* physical body of Jesus of Nazareth was resurrected on Easter morning. Let us therefore first briefly recall the results of Rudolf Steiner's research in relation to the particular nature of the resurrection body which rises from the grave at first light on Easter Sunday.

The resurrection body formed during the descent of the Son of God into the depths of the earth between Good Friday and Easter Sunday, is firstly constituted by the Christ spirit born into the earth at the moment that the body of Jesus Christ enters death. Secondly it also arises through transformation of the physical and etheric limbs of the Nathan (St Luke) Jesus,* who died on the Cross and is taken up into the earth in the night between Easter Saturday and Easter Sunday. From these two constituents the resurrection body is woven; in other words from what constitutes the physical human body, but is now penetrated with a divine spirit that passes through human death to conquer it. What, in this context, does it mean to 'conquer death'? This refers to spiritualized human nature, which was once unsullied by the adversary powers and can

---

* See, for example, Rudolf Steiner: *The Spiritual Guidance of the Individual and Humanity* (Anthroposophic Press 1992).

become so once again.* Rudolf Steiner describes the
formation of the resurrection body as a 'complete re-
establishment of the human being's lost evolutionary principles'.† If such a principle is 'lost' it
must once have been present. Through Christ's
sacrifice the human being's physical organization
was returned to the condition it had *before* the
influences of Lucifer and Ahriman took effect.‡

In future the human being is to become physically
'intact' again, as he once was before leaving paradise
– as he was physically *before* he was submerged in
the physical world and thus became mortal. The
physical condition he possessed before this Fall is
the state in which he will again depart from the
earth. This is the reason why Paul speaks of the

---

* Central to this view, and a core tenet of anthroposophy, is the
idea of reincarnation of the evolving human spirit as it develops
through the accumulated experiences of many earthly lives.
(Editor's note.)

† See the lecture of 11 October 1911 in *From Jesus to Christ*
(Rudolf Steiner Press 2005).

‡ Lucifer and Ahriman are the two polar forces of evil in
anthroposophical cosmology. Lucifer tempts us away from the
earth while Ahriman fetters us to it. Christ is the balancing
mediator between these two. (Editor's note.)

reality of Christ's resurrection as the 'second Adam'
(I. Corinthians, 15,47).

We could ask why the human being's spiritual
form had to become material at all, and encounter
Lucifer and Ahriman in a way that rendered us
mortal, if we are going to return once again to a
divine state.

The human being had to leave paradise because
the conditions under which he will be able to return
to the world of spirit are necessarily wholly different
from those in which he departed from it. The aim of
the good gods is to enable other beings, for instance
the human race, to become gods too. But a being can
only become divine if it does not need to be led and
guided by higher beings. During the period generally referred to as paradise, the dependent human
being was continually guided by the world of the
gods. Thus the human being gradually had to
release himself from his body-bound contact with
the world of spirit and thus also from his natural
clairvoyance. To make himself independent he had
to forget everything, sundering himself from his
God-given relationship to the spiritual world — he

had to turn to materialism so as, initially, to attain self-knowledge and, ultimately, develop his I. Thus we can say that the work of Lucifer and Ahriman in pre-Christian times was of definite service to the human being in developing his awareness, and this was allowed by the high spiritual hierarchies.

However, a time came when the influences of the dark powers grew too powerful. The I, present to begin with only in germinal form — and given to the human being by the Elohim only once he had descended to earth — was not able to master the astral body which was becoming ever stronger under Lucifer's influence, and which the human being had been developing ever since the Moon stage of evolution.* The consequence was a decadent path of evolution. The luciferic astral body began to influence the etheric body, and the latter, in turn, started to grow sclerotic — as did also, therefore, the physical body. At the turning point of time this evolutionary development was already inscribed into the

---

* See later passages in this volume for a description of the planetary incarnations which preceded and will succeed our 'Earth' stage of evolution. (Editor's note.)

face and form of some people. People who had undergone little or no higher development began to grow 'animalized'.

This does not mean they became like a normal animal. We owe our development into human beings to the animals, which remained behind at a lower level to allow human evolution to advance.* The animal evolved as far as the astral body and thus exists in the world in a natural condition with its three 'bodies' (physical, etheric and astral). It was not endowed with the I. But if the human being who has been given the disposition to work out of his I falls back to the level of the animal, to the astral, this represents the demise of the higher human being. With the degree of consciousness that the human being was able to acquire through his 'I' disposition, he had already become to some degree responsible for his actions in the pre-Christian era. The excessive power and egocentric use of his astral drives meant that the I-endowed person was able to do far

---

* See, for example, the lecture by Steiner on 29 January 1906 in *Original Impulses for the Science of the Spirit* (Completion Press 2001).

greater harm than an animal ever could. This began to come to the fore at the time of Christ, and the Redeemer's torturers — mostly mercenaries in the Jerusalem Temple Guard or the Roman army — already showed this kind of decadence in their features. During the Renaissance, at the beginning of the consciousness soul age,* these characteristics were brought to light by some painters in the flagellation or Cross-bearing scenes (see colour plates).

When people at the time of Christ died, they encountered the unbounded power of Ahriman, in whose realm a certain part of their being had to remain. This ahrimanic power beyond the threshold, the power of Ahriman over souls between death and a new birth, compelled the Christ being to pass through death Himself, to descend into the abyss in order to redress this condition for humanity. Only

---

* Our current epoch, beginning with the Renaissance and continuing for about 2000 years, provides the conditions with which humanity as a whole can develop this higher soul capacity. The consciousness soul carries full, independent awareness of the soul nature of the human being and also serves as a bridge to an understanding of the spiritual. (Editor's note.)

there – in the kingdom of death – could Ahriman be laid in chains. And it was there that the God Himself must descend in order to give help. This was not something that Christ could do during His life on earth when dwelling in the body of Jesus.

Thus people at the turning point of time were excessively exposed and subjected to the influences of Lucifer and Ahriman. Rudolf Steiner repeatedly describes how initiates at the time knew and felt that the high divine guidance to which they had previously turned was no longer able to do anything that could have offered a real process of healing for mankind.

Ultimately a divine being had to descend to help the human I to come to real birth. And this could only be done by God Himself becoming human, taking on physical and material existence out of pure love for the human race, and not shying away from death. A divine being came who, by allowing his divine nature to flow into the human organization, was able to curb the influence of Lucifer on human beings alive on the earth; and who banished Ahriman's power over human beings beyond the threshold of death by allowing His divine nature to flow into the abysses of death.

This being was Christ. His loving sacrifice means that *every* human being — not only, as in pre-Christian times, the initiate with clairvoyant vision who represented a whole nation or tribe — is henceforth able to emancipate himself from evolutionary stagnation and enter into a direct, individual relationship with the world of spirit.

Thus people were granted the possibility of raising themselves back up to the divine state once more, to a spiritualized condition, but now through their *own* will and endeavour. The corresponding 'apparel' which the human being wears in doing so, is the newly spiritualized physical sheath or resurrection body.

And thus we approach an understanding of the particular quality of the resurrection body which, since Christ's deed, can be 'put on' by each and every person who turns to the Christ being, at least in an initial, tentative form.* The commentary in

---

* See Rudolf Steiner's lectures *From Jesus to Christ* (Rudolf Steiner Press 2005).

this volume in relation to the spear wound aims to contribute another piece of the jigsaw to help understand the nature of this corporeality.

The occult background to the three earthquakes

On the resurrection body of Christ we find the four wounds of the Crucifixion: on hands and feet, and the spear wound to His side. But this body does not reveal the terrible wounds he sustained from torture and falling. Why do we see the one but not the other? We can and should ask such questions. Only when we have a question can we ever, eventually, arrive at real knowledge.

To discover the profound sense of this mystery of the spear wound let us first look at some particular natural phenomena which occurred between Good Friday and Easter Sunday. These natural events are occult processes beyond the threshold that entered the realm of earthly expression and became accessible to human senses.

During the Mystery of Golgotha three earthquakes

took place at certain intervals.* The first occurred on
Friday at around three in the afternoon (local time),
the moment of Jesus' death. This was when the earth
took the Christ spirit into itself. The body of Jesus
entered death, while the Christ spirit descended into
the abyss in order to renew the body of the earth.

Good Friday 3 p.m.

Christ's
spirit

---

*I previously referred to this in my comments on the resur-
rection in the book *And If He Has Not Been Raised...*

The second quake took place in the night between Saturday and Sunday, at around 2 a.m. The earth again absorbed something, in this case the corpse of Jesus which, abandoned by the spirit, first remained on the Cross and was then laid to rest in a cave. At this hour of the night the corpse sank into a cleft in the rock, so that the women found only an empty grave when they arrived in the early morning.

Sunday 2 p.m.

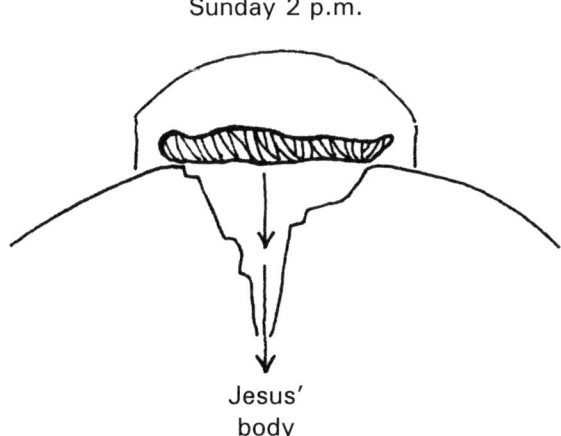

Jesus'
body

On the third occasion the earth quaked and opened – not in order to receive something, as it had previously when it received Christ's spirit on Friday and Jesus' body in the night before Sunday dawned, but this time to *release* something. The third earthquake took place at the moment of the resurrection on Sunday morning, around 6 a.m., when the resurrection body of Christ arose from the earth.

Dawn on Easter Sunday

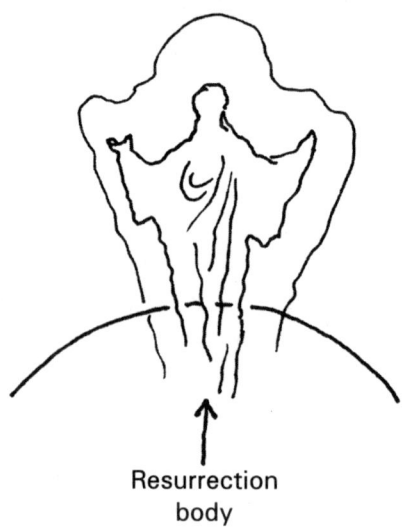

Resurrection
body

In the following observations on the mystery of the wounds of Christ, we will primarily examine the second earthquake. This comes as a powerful but very brief and sudden jolt in the night before the

Resurrection. The rock in the cave splits, receives the corpse, and closes again over it. This external phenomenon takes place as though in a moment of timelessness, of simultaneity. The rock opens and closes as though in a single instant. The continuum of earthly time is interrupted, which (among other things) also leads to the guards losing consciousness. When the uninitiated pass beyond the threshold – that is, into timelessness – they are torn out of normal waking consciousness.

This interruption of the continuum of earthly time occurs in relation to a particular occult process which I now want to examine.

At the moment of Jesus' death, the spirit of Christ unites with the earth, initiating the process described as the descent into the abyss or descent into hell. There the Christ spirit liberates from imprisonment by ahrimanic powers the souls that had entered death *before* the Christ event occurred. Through this release these souls for the first time experienced an expansion of their I beyond the threshold, and, for the first time since the earth began, gained vision of karmic connections. They were now able to work autonomously on their destiny beyond the threshold.

This upward expansion gradually led them level by level, through one earth stratum after another, upwards out of the underworld,* spreading outwards into cosmic planetary spheres. On their way, however, they also passed through those regions of the earth's surface where the flagellation, the Stations of the Cross and the Crucifixion had taken place. As each soul being in its upward flight penetrated these blood-soaked places, it received a direct experience of the suffering and thus of the sacrifice of Christ, even if it had not been in incarnation at the time this occurred. This passage of souls rising from the underworld though the places of Christ's passion occurred at the moment of the second earthquake.

With this second earthquake, when the earth opened and the corpse sank into it, something happened however which does not figure in sense-based historical tradition any more than the events described above. It is accessible only to inner vision,

---

* See the drawing in my book *And If He Has Not Been Raised . . .*, p. 80.

but is, nevertheless, historical in an occult sense. The souls liberated by Christ, who now spread outwards through the sacred places of the earth's surface, encountered spiritual hierarchies descending to these same places on earth. This simultaneous rising and descent of spiritual beings must be understood as linked with the 'non-temporal' opening and closing of the rock. Basically it occurred before the earthquake, yet everything also happened simultaneously, at the moment the earth opened. For what now occurred, as described below, can be ordered into a temporal sequence in normal human thinking, yet only because one thing appears as the consequence of another. Beyond the threshold, in contrast, inner connections such as cause and effect are not constrained in a temporal framework, since time, as it holds sway here on earth, need not be present there. Thus the actions of those beings of the hierarchies who went to the places of Jesus Christ's torments do, it is true, represent the conditions that gave rise to the opening of the rock and the assimilation of the corpse; but the intervention of the world of spirit in the earthly world is not in this case linked to the time continuum in which cause comes *before* effect. Everything occurred in a single, timeless moment; a timelessness enclosed by time.

What were these hierarchies doing? In a sacred act these beings of spirit – I would like to call them the servants, the retinue of the Exusiai, of the Elohim – gathered all the substances lost from the body of Jesus, left from the torture and falls, from all the grave injuries sustained during the stations of His path of suffering. They did not gather up the physical remains but the etheric part of these residues; the life forces from shreds of skin, blood, sweat and all physical substances that had belonged to the body of Jesus and had fallen upon the earth.

At the moment that the earthquake occurred, when the crucified body was taken into the earth, the hierarchies returned these etheric substances to the body. They filled the torture wounds again. This sacred gathering of the etheric substances of the body of Jesus was finished at the moment that the quake occurred – then the corpse could enter the earth, for it was now etherically complete.

The lost substances had to be returned to Jesus' etheric body, and with it be incorporated into the etheric body of the earth so that the earth could be entirely transformed. They became germinal etheric forces for the body of the earth. But that is only the task of *one part* of Jesus' etheric body, for it also had to play its part in the transformation of human nature into the resurrection body.

If we examine these occult historical events more closely we touch on something which – except through spontaneous intuition – can only be understood by means of spiritual science. The results or findings however, even without drawing on such means, can certainly be grasped with healthy human reason or with some knowledge of anthroposophy.

The diverse properties of different bodily sheaths

First it must be said that the fourfold human being is not constituted solely of four, self-contained, homogenous 'bodies' but that all four can be further inwardly differentiated and subdivided. For instance the human etheric body does not behave in a unified way during sleep. We know that the I and astral body detach themselves during sleep and rise up into cosmic regions. In general we say that during this phase the physical body remains lying in bed with the etheric body. But this is only a very general, simplified description of what really happens.

We can use simple means to show that the etheric body is not a unified entity. What we work on while awake with the help of the I can be imprinted into the lower bodies after death — but not only after death: to a certain degree this also occurs during sleep. Let us take an example to make this process more tangible. Imagine some vice or bad habit that we try to deal with, to rid ourselves of, such as smoking. This is something we don't necessarily have to pass through transformation after death to change. Stopping smoking is certainly something that can successfully be achieved within a single incarnation. So let us assume that smoking has become a bad habit in someone, has anchored itself deep in his etheric body. Now one day he decides to break this habit. Initially he uses his will to do so, to restrain his astral body, that is, his desire to smoke. He purges his astral body by means of his I. But it can happen — even if he has largely succeeded in accomplishing this soul purification — that he still reaches for a cigarette out of habit; and it can take months or even years until this last reflex has been banished from his etheric body. From such an example we can see how the astral can work upon the etheric. That it does so is clear from the fact that at some point a person no longer has the reflex impulse to reach for the cigarette pack.

The period during which the purging or purifying of the astral body is imprinted into the etheric body is the state of sleep (and in a similar way more extensive and significant work on the bodily sheaths is accomplished after death). However, the astral body during sleep can only imprint the results or fruits of the I's work into that part of the etheric body which, like the astral body itself, is *outside* the physical body. A part of the etheric body separates in sleep from the rest of the etheric body, and, side-by-side with the astral body, departs from the body. It is not true to say that the fruits of the work of the astral body are pressed into the etheric body when the former returns from the world of spirit on awakening, when it descends and reunites with the etheric body; but rather that a part of the etheric body – in this case we could call it the 'astral part' of the etheric body – separates from the physical body during sleep, along with the astral body, and thus expands to a much greater extent than the rest of the etheric body.

From this we can see that the etheric body can be differentiated into various parts. If it were not inwardly differentiated, if parts of it could not extend further beyond the threshold of the physical organism, there would scarcely be tangible effects proceeding from the I's work on the lower bodies within a single incarnation.

A further indication of this distinctive nature of the human etheric body is shown by the following: we know that the human being has been able to work upon and transform his three lower bodies through the I only since the Christ event, or no later than the dawn of the consciousness soul age.

Let us look at the etheric body once more. The work of the I transforms the etheric body to life spirit, to buddhi. But this does not occur all at once and completely. The human being does not wake up one morning and find he has developed buddhi. The I transforms the etheric body very gradually: first only parts of it, through life's varying experiences, through life's trials and through conscious practice. If we only had a homogenous, unified etheric body, we could not slowly and gradually develop buddhi. But the part of the etheric body that has been transformed within us, that we have transformed into buddhi through ongoing spiritual work and practice, is not lost to us after death, nor when we strive towards a new incarnation. This transformed part of the etheric body is reintegrated into our new etheric body, which we attract to ourselves through the help of the hierarchies.

When we die, our untransformed etheric passes into the earth's etheric, and thus nourishes the earth. It enters into a process of circulation. But the etheric forces we have transformed into buddhi through the power of the I can accompany the I, spreading beyond this etheric sphere. This part of our higher body is preserved and, with our I forces, is able to work alongside the first hierarchy on developing a new physical body for our forthcoming life on earth.

The earth as physical body of the Christ Spirit

Even the most sublimely developed etheric body of the Jesus body, into which the Christ was able to enter at the Jordan baptism, possesses diverse parts which fulfilled different tasks during the process of dying and after death. But development in the case of the Christ being, inasmuch as it united with the destiny of the earth, runs in the opposite direction to that of human beings.* While the human being rises into the spiritual cosmos after death, the Christ Spirit descends into the depths of the earth at the

---

* Rudolf Steiner spoke of this to some extent in his lectures published as *The Fifth Gospel* (Rudolf Steiner Press 1995).

death of Jesus. Rudolf Steiner describes this process as the true birth of Christ.

Thus a part of Jesus' etheric body enters the earth – the part, that is, which consists of the substances gathered back together and the remaining corporeal part. This is the part of the etheric body that in an ordinary human being one would call buddhi. After death this buddhi part expands to the cosmic sun because, through the work of the I, it does *not* pass into the spiritual composting process, that is, into the earth's ether. This transformed part of the etheric body is not lost in the etheric sphere as spiritual nutrient but it can – as an aspect of the I – take the same path through the planetary spheres as the immortal core of being, the I. But whereas the human being's higher etheric body is drawn as far as the sun, the etheric part of the Jesus body is drawn down to the centre of the earth.

We can ask why the etheric body of Jesus, made whole with the collected substances lost during His torments, does not also draw away from the earth towards the cosmic sun and the breadths of the cosmos.

The fact that one part of the etheric body of Jesus is drawn down into the earth is subject to a decisive condition: before the body sinks into the rock fissure in the night between Easter Saturday and Easter Sunday, the Christ Spirit has preceded it into the depths of the earth, having already departed from Jesus' body on Good Friday when death occurred at the Crucifixion. Through the descent of the Christ Spirit into the underworlds, in a certain sense the earth henceforth bears the sun within it. The descended Christ laid a sun seed into the inmost earth: the potential for it to become a sun itself in the future.

It is to this sun seed within the earth that this etheric part of the Jesus body goes, sinking down at the earthquake into the rock fissure before the Sunday dawn. It is drawn towards the Christ sun within the earth. And this part of the etheric body, the buddhi part, helps in the Christ Spirit's work of drawing towards it a new – in fact His first and only – *physical* body: the earth body, the earth itself (see drawing on page 47).

A certain part of Christ's resurrection body is

The journey of the human being

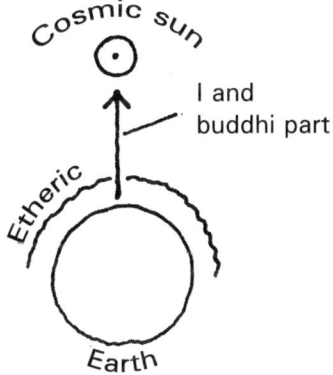

The journey of Christ

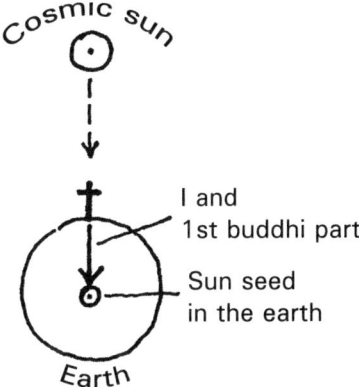

thereby created as potential. To recreate the human being's archetypal physical form, the pure, transfigured and at the same time *complete* body of formative forces of Jesus was needed. This part of the resurrection body is connected with the human being's earthly nature, for since the latter was created it has been able, step-by-step, and corresponding to human spiritual development, to spiritualize itself also. The special characteristic of this constituent of the resurrection body is to endow the earthly form of the human being with the life it needs on the likewise evolving earth. Jesus' healed body of formative forces was essential to this evolution. And the entry of this body into the earth, and fulfilment of its lofty task, was made possible by the deed of the hosts of the Exusiai, by their gathering and returning of the etheric substances lost from the body of Jesus during the Passion. This is why the torture wounds are not carried over into the archetypal image of the physical body, the so-called phantom or resurrection body, for these wounds were filled again by the gathering and reincorporation of lost etheric substance.

The Crucifixion wounds and renewal of the earth's aura

These statements relate, however, only to one part of the Redeemer's etheric body. Let us now look at the other part of His etheric body, which enters the aura of the earth already from the Cross. As the Redeemer's blood flows from the nail wounds, the earth's etheric sphere is transformed in an instant. Rudolf Steiner describes this in moving terms in his lectures on the Fifth Gospel.* The blood that flows from the wounds touches the earth and renews its encircling aura before the Christ Spirit undergoes earthly death (see drawing on page 50).

The sacrifice of Christ, connected with the nail wounds, consists on the one hand of allowing luciferic influences on human nature to bleed away — in other words, of purifying the blood as bearer of the I; and on the other hand it consists of the descent of God Himself into the realm of Ahriman.

---

* See in particular the lecture on 10 February 1914 in *The Fifth Gospel* (Rudolf Steiner Press 1995).

Good Friday before 3 p.m.

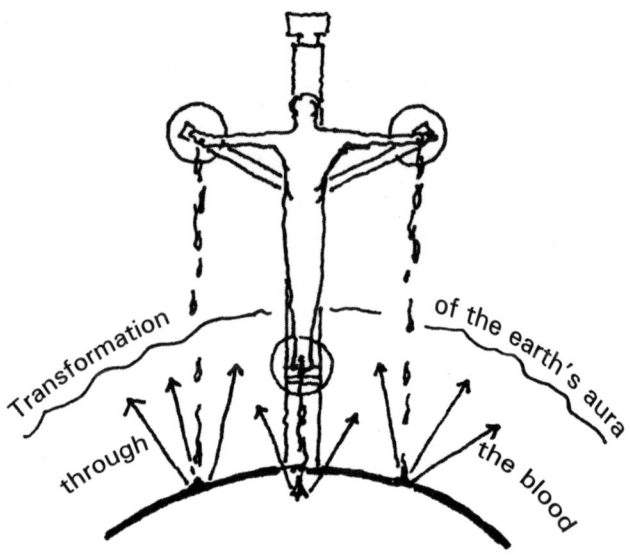

The nail wounds allow the body's purification from Lucifer, and the liberation from Ahriman after death. As testimony that the dark powers have been vanquished, the victory seal of the Crucifixion wounds is impressed into the archetype of the physical body, so that the resurrection body bears the signs of these wounds. The resurrection body is of course free from the influences of these powers. The wound marks accentuate the places through which the physical archetype of the human being was purified of the influences of the adversary powers. This phenomenon also highlights the properties of the resurrection body, for in a certain sense it is not a 'new' body that is created, but rather the purged, cleansed, *renewed* archetypal human physical body. This is why Paul, as we have already mentioned, speaks of the 'second' or 'last' Adam when he refers to the loss of Adam's archetypal form (I. Corinthians 15, 45–47), which he had prior to the Fall and expulsion from paradise, that is, before his submersion in a material bodily form.

The wound marks are the places where etheric forces stream out to renew the earth's aura, and through them the human body was purged of the destructive influences of adversary forces. This is why the nail wounds were not 'refilled', fulfilling as they do the high occult task of transforming the earth's ether sphere through the outflowing of the blood.

A simple schematic picture – which must be seen as a mere schema rather than a precise reflection of the actuality – can help us grasp the two special aspects of Jesus' etheric body as described above, together with their divine purpose. Both aspects participate in development of the resurrection body (see drawing below).

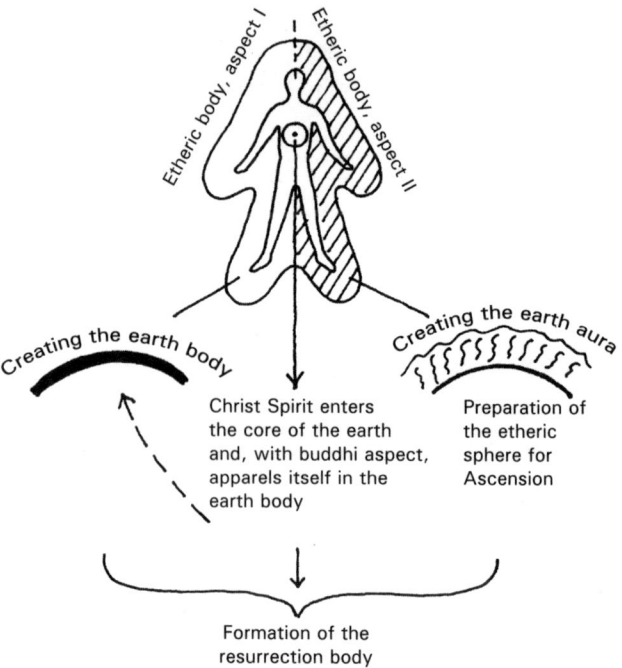

Etheric body, aspect I

Etheric body, aspect II

Creating the earth body

Creating the earth aura

Christ Spirit enters
the core of the earth
and, with buddhi aspect,
apparels itself in the
earth body

Preparation of
the etheric
sphere for
Ascension

Formation of the
resurrection body

First, while still on the Cross, the earth's aura is renewed. Here an ether sphere is created that is necessary for the renewal of the earth body —

which is simultaneously the true birth of Christ —
after the death of Jesus. It is like the birth of a
human being: in a first stage the human I and soul
draw towards them an appropriate etheric body.
In a second stage the human being can then take
on a fitting physical form. On the Cross, the out-
flow of purified blood from the nail wounds first
renews the earth's etheric body. Only then can the
deity's physical body be added to this. This physical body of the deity is the earth body. The *earth
ether* becomes Christ's *etheric body* on Good
Friday, and subsequently the *earth body* becomes
Christ's *physical body.*

For the resurrection body this means that it rises
from the grave without any trace of torture or tor-
ment. This can occur through the holy occult deed
accomplished by the hierarchies of the sun sphere,
who complete and perfect that part of Jesus' etheric
body which draws towards it the physical body for
the Christ Spirit, that is, the earth body. In contrast,
the nail wounds as openings for overcoming the
adversary powers ray out from the recreated phantom. At these places the I pushes outwards the other

aspect of the etheric body, which was responsible for renewing the earth's aura.*

The earth's aura was prepared and formed anew through the blood flowing from the Cross so as to enable the resurrection body of the Lord to be absorbed into it on the day of Ascension. This entry of the resurrection body into the earth's aura on Ascension day created the conditions for multiplication of the resurrection corporeality during the ten days between Ascension and Whitsun. Since the first Whitsun it has been possible for each person to attract the germinal spark of his own, individually distinctive, resurrection body. Thus each and every person, through the entry of the first resurrection body into the earth's aura on the original Ascension day, has acquired the potential for an individual spirit-body form.† Nowadays people direct their gaze to this sphere when they perceive Christ in the

---

* Comments made by Rudolf Steiner about the blood flowing from the Cross relate to the purification of the astral body; in this present volume attention is focused solely on the role of the etheric body.

† See the lecture given on 14 May 2005 in my book *And If He Has Not Been Raised . . .*

etheric. The spiritual organ which people of the present and future are beginning to develop, is one that belongs to this resurrection body. It has the same 'substantiality', the same quality as the resurrection body: in other words, it is an etheric organ. This etheric eye perceives within the sphere to which it belongs, the etheric sphere; and it is therefore constituted in such a way that it can discern the presence of Christ in the etheric being of the earth, and His unity with it.

The holy, diligent gathering of traces of the etheric body by the spiritual hierarchies, and the returning of these substances to the Jesus body, thus occurs in the night before Sunday during the second earthquake, when the body of Jesus is absorbed into the earth through the rock fissure. The Jesus body, like the Christ Spirit, penetrates to the core of the earth, but must not be confused with it. Christ Himself descended to the abysses of earth at the moment Jesus died on the Cross, whereas the body of Jesus was only taken up by the earth at the moment the spiritual conditions were created to allow it to serve renewal of the phantom. This moment arrived when

the power of the ahrimanic hosts had been vanquished to an extent that ensured they could no
longer triumph over matter. The body of Jesus not
only had to enter the earth unscathed, but *remain* in
the same intact state, undamaged by the influence of
Ahriman in the earth, so that the spiritualization of
corporeality could occur.

II

THE SPEAR-WOUND MYSTERY AND THE
GRAIL BLOOD

The mystery of the spear wound points us towards spiritualization of the physical body. The special, pure elixir that flows from the side of the Lord is certainly an exoteric reference to an esoteric process of development that occurred – for the first time, yet symptomatically for all human beings – here on earth within the space of a few hours. (We need to counter the idea that spiritual processes and the higher developments they bring about unfold exclusively beyond the threshold, and never impinge on the sensory word. It is an erroneous gnostic mode of thought that regards the Christ sacrifice, His transformation and resurrection, as a process solely of spirit and soul. This would be a denial of Paul's teaching. What use is spiritual development if it has no reforming effect on the lower bodies? And these lower bodies – particularly the lowest, the physical body – belong to the earthly world and can only be worked upon during incarnation. All development in the spirit aims to enliven the mortal human being. All higher spiritual development at the same time works and impinges on matter. Serious spiritual work always leads to deed and action in the physical world. The appearance of a divine being in the material world embodied this to the very highest degree.)

The spear-wound mystery is one of transformation, of etherization; and it takes place before the eyes of those present at the time. One of these witnesses became a source of truth for us, leaving his testimony in the form of the Gospel of St John. If this Gospel by the disciple whom the Lord loved is read in the right way it reveals to us deep truths about the Mystery of Golgotha, which today can be taken up in a new way and understood through anthroposophical spiritual science.

The testimony of St John

St John points us with clear, in fact unmistakable, words to the extraordinary, stirring circumstances which arose when the spear wound occurred:

> *But one of the soldiers with a spear pierced his side, and forthwith came there out blood and water. And he that saw bare record, and his record is true: and he knoweth that he saith true, that ye might believe.* (John, 19, 34 f.)

The formulation and reference to the truth of the testimony is unusual. The author emphasizes three times that he witnessed this: he says that he saw the spear wound given, and that his testimony is true. Why, in this passage, does John give a threefold assurance of its truth? He does so because he knows he is speaking of two facts that are completely out of the ordinary, which a person with normal, merely sensory, earthly experience must regard as fantasy. He wants to make sure no one thinks he was either mistaken, expressed himself in a way that could be misunderstood, or even expressed himself wrongly. And indeed the reader of the Gospel is deeply shaken by these occult facts that are made manifest right down into the physical realm.

What people in the fourth cultural epoch still had to accept through faith alone can no longer remain an inexplicable miracle for us in the consciousness soul age. From the wound in the Lord's side blood pours forth, although death had already occurred. More precisely, the corpse of Jesus had been hanging on the Cross for about an hour before the spear wound was given. Even those unversed in medical science know that blood can only flow from a wound when the blood is circulating: that is, during life. The second peculiar phenomenon, to which St John points with such emphasis, is the fact that *water* also flowed out along with the blood.

Let us turn our attention for a while to historical events at the time of Christ, and describe them in somewhat more detail than was possible in the Gospels. A great individuality, of whom I intend to speak in a wider context and greater detail, is connected with the spear-wound mystery, which can also be called a Grail mystery. This is Joseph of Arimathea, who had witnessed the Crucifixion at some distance from the hill of Golgotha. When the Redeemer had finally reached the end of His bitter, tormented path of suffering, Joseph went immediately to Pontius Pilate to ask him for Jesus' corpse.

Without more ado Pilate released the corpse. The reason for this was the unpleasantness he had experienced in connection with the condemning of Jesus. Joseph of Arimathea found Pilate in a shocking mental and physical state, for only a few minutes previously there had been an earthquake in Jerusalem and the sky had grown dark. Thousands of people ran panic-stricken through the streets. Pilate had ordered some of the city gates to be shut and had sent further troops to the crucifixion hill, but some soldiers had also fled in fear. Hundreds of people were cursing Pilate for passing sentence of death on Jesus of Nazareth, for probably everyone was rightly making a connection between the suffering and death of Jesus and the fearful natural phenomena accompanying it. Pilate was now on the one hand fearful of a rebellion that would have endangered his career, and on the other hand he was inwardly shaken and alarmed that his judgement might lead the vengeful gods to inflict some stroke of destiny on him. Above all he felt the cunning arguments of the high priests had persuaded him to pass the sentence, and had put him in this precarious position, and he was irritated and annoyed by this.

However, he knew that the high priests wanted to have the body of Jesus thrown into a common grave with the other felons. This measure of denying a dead person or his family a proper burial was the worst form of humiliation for the Jewish people in the culture of those days. Jewish funerary rites were something special since they were connected with the expectation of the coming of the Messiah. The kinds of graves common in Jewish tradition up to the time of Christ really only existed because the Messiah would one day arise from such a grave; the prophets had foretold this.

Thus Joseph of Arimathea's request was welcome to Pilate inasmuch as he knew that releasing the corpse of Jesus would go a little way towards revenging himself on the high priests; and at the same time he was hoping to placate the gods by doing this.

In the meantime, however, some mercenaries of the temple army had already been sent to Golgotha to break the legs of those who had been crucified, so that they would die more swiftly. No one wanted to leave the crucified hanging there throughout the Sabbath, due to start at sunset of that day. These temple soldiers knew nothing of Pilate's order to release the corpse to Joseph of Arimathea, and intended to break the Lord's legs also. Only the greatest protest, commotion and exertions from relatives made them refrain from this. The temple soldiers did not believe that the wracked person whom they saw in front of them was already dead. They perceived some unnamed power in the body hanging on the Cross — something quite different from anything they were used to seeing in a dead body. These mercenaries were no doubt far from any capacity to cast an eye of spirit on the Redeemer, and yet their first, spontaneous, impression told them there was still life in him!

This seemingly unimportant detail directs our attention to the divine spirit working right down into the physical in a way that could even be perceived by people who stood firmly in a merely sensory grasp of the world.

At the protests of Jesus' relatives, the temple soldiers left the body and moved on to the still-living felons, breaking their arms, legs and ribcages so that they died immediately.

At some distance a Roman Soldier named Cassius — later known as Longinus — had witnessed the commotion surrounding the intended breaking of the bones. Shortly after Jesus' death he had been elevated to the rank of captain because the previous bearer of this post, an officer named Abn Adar, had recognized the Son of God in the dead 'Joshua', and had immediately renounced his office. Quite abruptly, as though governed by an alien impetus, and initially unnoticed by all those present, he took his spear and rode his horse decisively up the crucifixion hill. His deed, which he fulfilled upon the body of the Lord, took place in a few seconds; and yet it seemed that time stood still. He pierced the body with his full strength, from a lower right-hand angle through the ribcage, lung, and into the heart. Then he tore the spear out of the side of the corpse again with a mighty pull, and the bright blood of the Redeemer gushed forth powerfully, pouring at the foot of the Cross into a depression of greenish rock where it foamed and was contained. Jesus's loved ones cried out in horror, pain and compassion, but when they saw the blood, this living, foaming blood which shone like the sun, all were transformed in an instant. Cassius too – as if awakening from a deep sleep – appeared illumined, and fierily professed his faith in the living Son of God. The relatives, as if on the impulse of a higher power, rushed to the natural Grail cup of the rock to catch the living blood, which they preserved in vessels and skins that were quickly brought.

What does all this mean? What is the unique property of the blood that flows from the wound in the Lord's side? Let us examine the phenomena from anthroposophical perspectives so as to meet the Grail blood mystery with greater understanding.

The evolution and higher evolution of the body

What constitutes us as spiritual beings – in other words what makes us fully human – lives, as we know, in the element of warmth. The human I lives in the blood, in its heat, through which it is borne into our physical nature. The blood was also the first element which made the human being into an earthly being.

Next closest to the human spirit is the element of air, the second aspect indwelling us as we became human beings on earth. After endowing us with blood warmth, the Exusiai breathed the divine breath of life into us. Only subsequently did we link with the watery element. While we pass through earthly life this endows the physical body with formative, structuring forces. The human body consists of 75 per cent water. The mineral element, finally, is the furthest removed from the human spirit. From the mineral realm we have our bones, the whole physical sheath in which our earthly sojourn unfolds.

The elements affected on the Cross, which were transformed through the nailing and binding of the body, were the warmth and air element: blood and breath. These two I-permeated elements of blood and air, which the human being had once received from the Elohim,* were refashioned on the Cross through the death of the Redeemer as representative of all humanity. This took place through the binding of Jesus with ropes and knots — which was accompanied by transformation of the breath — and through the nail wounds, from which humanity's lust- and passion-driven blood flowed out. Cassius pierced the organic bearers of these elements, the lung and heart.

If we read what Rudolf Steiner has to say about the Rosicrucian path of initiation, we find that two steps on this path are the preparation of the Philosophers' Stone and Attainment of the Grail.† These two stages of initiation mutually determine each other and, in a certain way, affect each other's realization and effect. This gives expression to the fact that in future the human being will no longer expel

---

* In connection with Jesus Christ's cry on the Cross of 'Eli, Eli, lema sabachthani!' I have previously spoken of the role of the Elohim who once endowed the human being with blood and breath. See the lecture of 12 December 2004 in the book *And If He Has Not Been Raised*...

† See Rudolf Steiner's lectures in *Rosicrucian Wisdom* (Rudolf Steiner Press 2000).

carbon into his environment but oxygen, thus consciously transforming his body in the same way that plants already do so without consciousness. At the same time we will develop the organ which produces this breath and thus also the word. In other words we will transform the larynx.

In passing let me say that the larynx really belongs to the human trunk. It is assigned to the heart-lung organization, though it extends into the head which it will be able to loosen and open up through its future transformation.

This transformed larynx, the spoken word that streams forth from it, will make it possible in future to give life to another I. The larynx will become a new, wholly chaste organ of reproduction.*

But the prerequisite for this is that the human being's lowest, mineralized body is raised one level higher into the etheric. Our lowest sheath partakes of the mineral realm, composed of all that constitutes the mineral parts of the physical body, such as bones, flesh and everything that decomposes.

---

* Ibid., lecture dated 6 June 1907.

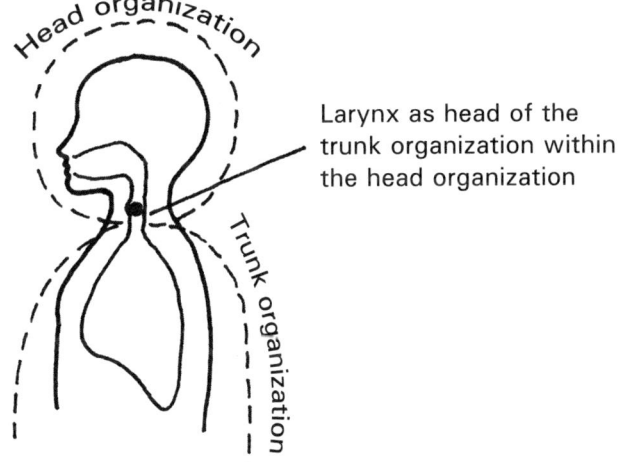

Larynx as head of the trunk organization within the head organization

The lowest level of the spiritual hierarchies, on the other hand, is not the mineral realm but the etheric. The human being is striving to evolve towards this condition, for by the planetary incarnation of the Jupiter earth he will have potentially attained this angelic stage. The human being who creates through the word, as described in the Rosicrucian path of development, will have raised his mineral aspect into a fluid one, that is into the etheric sphere.

Drawing on the earth's evolutionary history we can clarify this process. In Rudolf Steiner's *Occult*

*Science** we find a detailed description of the condition of the earth at the 'Saturn' stage as a spiritual
warmth condition. When the earth planet then
passed through the Sun stage this became an air
condition, then subsequently a new, fluid state
during the Moon stage. Only during the current
stage of planetary embodiment, the Earth stage,† did
a mineral realm come into existence.

In our life here on earth, in this mineral kingdom,
we can also say that our language developed a
'mineral' conceptual world. When we speak of
warmth, air and water conditions during earlier
evolutionary stages, such concepts are drawn
entirely from a material and mineral context. But
really we need to develop quite different ideas, for
instance of the warmth condition on Saturn, than
those we usually have in mind when we think of
'warmth' or 'heat'. Where no matter exists to absorb
and reflect heat, we need to conceive of warmth in a

---

* R. Steiner: *Occult Science, An Outline* (Rudolf Steiner Press
1969), in the chapter 'Man and the Evolution of the World'.
† 'Earth' with an initial capital refers throughout to the present
stage in the sequence of planetary incarnations rather than the
physical planet itself. (Editor's note.)

wholly different way. We have therefore already spoken of 'soul' and spiritual warmth,* for the physical aspect present on Saturn was not in fact material in nature. The same applies to all other conditions in which the mineral realm as we know it today did not yet exist When we now describe how in future the human being will transform his physical being from a solid to a fluid state, this is simply sensory language to express the fact that he will raise his physical state from a mineral to an etheric condition.

In the future three planetary conditions of the earth, human evolution will lead us back into an increasingly spiritualized state, in contrast to our evolution up to the Mystery of Golgotha which led us into deepening materialization. Specifically this means that the Jupiter stage will acquire a more Moon-like quality of embodiment; and that of Venus, as we advance to a more spiritual state, will tend more towards a gaseous condition. The Vulcan planetary condition, in the furthest future, will be

---

* See *Occult Science, An Outline*, 'Man and the Evolution of the World.'

wholly comparable with the warmth state of Saturn. The decisive difference here is, however, that the human being will *himself* initiate this transformation, whereas his whole descent from the spiritual warmth condition of Saturn to the mineral, earthly realm was intended solely to endow him with the capacity to make this return ascent by his own means.

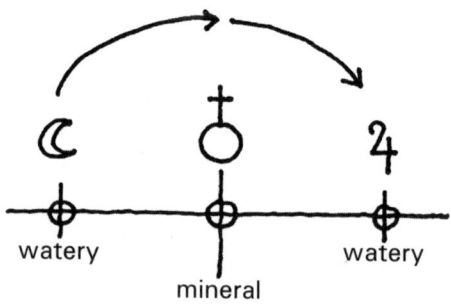

The process of spiritualization of our mineral aspect into a watery condition may initially appear very odd, or at least difficult to imagine. But consider for a moment human evolution on the earth today and in the future, as the Rosicrucian path describes it: today a human embryo swims in the watery environment of the mother's womb after conception. Conception and all maturation takes place in this fluid element. In the future this process will rise one stage higher. Then the child will be 'spoken into existence' by means of the transformed larynx, being conceived in the will-directed medium of air.

Today the physical body of the reproductive human being is interwoven with the mineral kingdom, whereas the development of a new human being takes place in the fluid realm. In future the human being's physical body will have acquired a 'fluid' state, but will conceive the child in a gaseous-type element through the higher word, with the larynx. Thus the whole process of existence and reproduction is raised one stage higher.

The reason the 'fluid' state is placed in inverted commas is that we must take account here of the conceptual difficulty referred to above. As described, the concept 'water' or 'fluid' stands in our sensory-based language and understanding for the *etheric* realm one stage higher than the mineral. Etheric formative forces are present today in the fluid parts of earthly human beings. In the mineral world the etheric is expressed as the 'fluid' condition.

The etherized blood: the renewed basis of life

Let us recall once again the testimony of St John. He bears witness to the fact that not only blood but also *water* poured forth when Cassius pierced the Redeemer's lung and heart. And, as can be confirmed from direct experience, this water was not just a little tissue fluid but brightly foaming, spurting blood: in other words, a considerable quantity of fluid.*

Something, therefore, gave the blood a physical basis for life, although the old physical body, the

---

* In his picture 'Damnation and Salvation', Lukas Kranich the elder points to this mystery of the flow and enlivening of the blood, depicting a horizontal spurt of blood coming from the side wound. Even though the blood did not pour out in this way, but rather in a mighty, living gush, it does, nevertheless, highlight the Grail blood mystery of the living blood pouring forth from a dead body and, due to the increased amount of water in it, spurting in a uniquely fluid way. See for example the illustration in *And If He Has Not Been Raised...*

mineral body, was dead. This foundation of life was the watery element. And St John speaks of 'water' because it is the sensory expression of the etheric. The water was clearly the bearer of the living blood. This blood was able to be as alive in the watery element as it had previously been in the mineral realm, in the mineral body of Jesus of Nazareth. Thus water and blood are in the same mutual relationship as bread and wine at the Last Supper — that is body and blood. The water as such, which pours from the spear wound, is the densified manifestation of the etheric in the mineral realm.

Cassius *had* to open the Lord's side, for the old body was no more the place to preserve the etherized blood of the future than the grave was the fitting receptacle for the resurrection body. We can certainly draw this parallel. On the morning of the resurrection the angels said to the women: 'Why seek ye the living amongst the dead? He is not here!' And likewise a new medium other than the dead, mineral body, had to form the new vessel for the new blood.

This blood was able to be transformed by the Holy

Spirit which had descended into the Jesus body at the Jordan baptism. For three years the Christ Spirit worked in this body, first as a kind of 'guest', very loosely connected and moving from one disciple to another. Only in death did the Christ Spirit unite in the most intensive way with the Jesus body, so that we can then truly speak of the Son of Man. After this period of three years, the Christ Spirit had wholly penetrated and permeated the physical body of Jesus, had imbued it so thoroughly that in it He could pass through human death. This work of the I — and the Holy Spirit may well be called the essence of all 'I's — leaves traces in what constitutes a major part of the physical body: the blood.

On the Cross the Lord did actually 'give up the ghost': at the moment of death the Spirit of Christ departed from the body of Jesus in order to embark on His life in the earth's interior. He withdrew from this mineral body and no longer permeated it. But the blood transformed by the Christ I remained in this body. The Spirit of Christ no longer worked within this body in a way that maintained its life, but He had previously worked upon the blood so that this could retain its life independently of the old body.

This is why the temple soldiers were unsure whether the Lord was already dead. They still discerned signs of life in the wracked body bound to the Cross, and therefore wanted to break the legs to be certain.

But once the transformation of the blood had been accomplished, this new source of life could not possibly remain trapped in the old body. 'Why seek ye the living amongst the dead?' The new blood did not belong to the old body. Thus Cassius fulfilled the divine plan. His seemingly shocking intervention in fact liberated the elixir of humanity from the sclerotic physical constraints of the past, from the chains of death. Only through his courageous deed, the spear stroke, did life pour out into the world. The transformed blood of life no longer belonged in the old, mineral vessel, and was freed on the Cross through the deed of Cassius-Longinus. It is inconceivable that it would have been buried with the body.

Thus, during the historical hour of time between

death and the spear wound there was blood in the
dead, mineral, physical body on the Cross at Golgotha which could remain alive without this body.
The water to which St John bears witness is the
etheric, the basis of the new *physical* human being. It
formed what was now the lowest level of physical
life. That is why the etherized blood could break
forth in a living way independently of the old body.

The transformed, purified blood of the representative of humanity, the I-bearer, will in future
flow within an element that tends towards the fluid.
Just as our blood today still penetrates the mineral
and physical realm, so in future it will pulse through
the physical etheric.

We must be quite clear that, while a physical body
is bound to matter during an earth incarnation, it is
never solely material in nature. In future it will not
inevitably be bound to mineral constituents. The
conditions we have already described in the case of
the Moon stage of our planetary body will be more
or less the state of physical existence in the further
course of earth evolution – at that stage which we
call the Jupiter earth (see drawing on page 72).

The physical body at the etheric level

Rudolf Steiner himself engaged in a long process of research in relation to the properties of the resurrection body. In 1911 he put forward the concept of the resurrection body, or phantom, and spoke about its deep significance. In previous years he gave a series of lectures in which he was visibly wrestling with the difficulties of characterizing this mystery. He described this form of the new human being as a kind of special etheric body. In his Apocalypse lecture series, given in Nuremberg in 1908, he was still putting it as follows when referring to Paul's words:

> 'It is sown in corruption; it is raised in incorruption.' The incorruptible body will then be resurrected. 'It is sown a natural body; it is raised a spiritual body.' Paul calls the etheric or life body the 'spiritual body' after the physical has dissolved and the etheric body enters the astral earth. Here Paul is foreseeing the incorruptible spiritual body, as he calls it.*

---

* In the lecture given on 26 June 1908, in *The Apocalypse of St John* (Anthroposophic Press 1993).

This way of putting it is certainly striking, particularly if we reflect on Rudolf Steiner's later ideas and insights. This 'etheric body' possessed 'all the properties of the *physical* body' as Rudolf Steiner later recognized,* for it represented the recreation of the human being's intact *physical* organization.

And so we can say that what we are describing is not a 'normal' *etheric body* but a *physical body* at the etheric level. The resurrection body is a *physical* body raised and developed from the mineral into the etheric realm: the physical body of future human beings, and of the same etheric quality as the Grail blood that poured forth from the side of the Lord.

And this is also how we must understand the Grail blood, none of which could be buried alive. And so all the blood that was contained in this body flowed out of it: around four to five litres of living, foaming blood poured into the basin of rock at the foot of the Cross. We have already said that this rock was green in colour. But this was not so beforehand. Before the holy blood touched the stone it was

---

* See lecture given on 11 October 1911 in *From Jesus to Christ* (Rudolf Steiner Press 2005).

yellowish-white in colour, like all the other rocks in Jerusalem. When the living blood touched it, however, the rock sank down, forming a vessel-like basin, and changing its colour to green.

When considering the events connected with the Mystery of Golgotha we must repeatedly recall that at no other moment of earth evolution did the spiritual manifest so directly in the material world as at this time of Christ. This is wholly understandable. Through creation of the first purified blood by the representative of humanity, and of the first purified physical body, a completed, concluded stage of evolution entered the earthly world as though from the future, in exemplary fashion: a state that humanity will still take many millennia to achieve. During the three days of the Mystery of Golgotha a radiant, luminous embodiment of truth was given to humanity so that it could know what it must evolve into. A blood and a body whose lowest, living aspect was not in the mineral kingdom came into being archetypally in the mineral kingdom, prefiguring a condition within this mineral kingdom which in its natural — that is etheric — environment would not have appeared as anything out of the ordinary. But where this future condition extends back as it were into a present, imperfect state, it seems out of place. And now, of course, when this future quality intervenes at one stroke in present circumstances, or is suddenly present within them, it has the power to transform what is backward in comparison with it. Wherever spiritually developed or future currents touch the present, they draw less evolved contemporary aspects into them and transform them.

Thus the mineral, the rock on Golgotha, became soft as plant substance when it came into contact with the etherized blood, and at the same time it took on a green colour, similar to that we can observe in plants. If we turn an eye of spirit to the nature of the plant, we can see that the green colour perceived with the physical eye shows the same colour character in the etheric realm. The green of plants is, in fact, the only sensory colour shade which is the same as the 'spiritual' colour of the plant — that is, its etheric expression. And thus, on contact with the Grail blood, the rock was raised to a level corresponding to it. Rock became, in the deepest sense, plant-like. At that place the mineral kingdom became raised wholly into the etheric realm.

Through the centuries the blood flowing from the Redeemer's side, the Grail blood, was always assigned the property of giving eternal life. Anthroposophical spiritual science can certainly validate this view through its insight into spiritual realities and relationships. Whoever knows the secret of the Grail blood has the key to understanding eternal life. Those who, in persistent dedication to the high goal of humanity, strive in the light of the Christ being, and never turn away from suffering, will develop this purified blood within their own organism. From incarnation to incarnation they will gradually apparel themselves in the resurrection body of Christ and eventually — seen from the level of the mineral kingdom — no longer die in an old body. Then they will have 'eternal' life. John describes this stage in his Apocalypse with the words: 'Blessed and holy are they who partake of this resurrection: on them the second death shall have no power' (Revelations 20,6).

Even before 1911, when he finally found a conceptual language to describe the mystery of the blood and the resurrection body, Rudolf Steiner said on one occasion: 'The spiritual overcame the purely physical attributes of the blood. Only when we do not regard the blood as composed of merely chemical constituents, as the materialist does, can we understand what occurred at Golgotha.'*

---

*In the lecture on 29 July 1906 in *The Christian Mystery* (Completion Press 2000).

III

THE STATIONS OF THE CROSS AND THE SEVEN WORDS OF CHRIST ON THE CROSS

In turning our attention to Christ's Stations of the Cross, our gaze will now be directed on the one hand to the historical sequence of events; but at the same time also — and this is why this account is connected with the spear-wound mystery — to the deeper esoteric significance of the Stations and Christ's suffering on the Cross up to the point of death. When we attend to the deeper meaning of these events, gain certain insights and try to communicate these, it may seem that our gaze is directed to a quite different context from that existing between the separate, externally demonstrable circumstances. If the aim is to draw attention from a spiritual-scientific perspective to a particular esoteric relationship between separate external occurrences, the chronological sequence of events can sometimes recede into the background. In the same way that the eye turns from a single flower to encompass the harmonious and aesthetic interplay of colours of a whole meadow, we will endeavour to understand the Stations of the Cross by considering them from a wider perspective and at odds with a purely chronological sequence, according to which they would have come *before* an account of the spear-wound mystery. The spear-wound on the Cross would never have occurred if Christ had not previously borne the Cross to Golgotha. But here the bearing of the Cross is to be examined retrospectively in its relationship to the spear wound. These historical events are in fact connected in a different way from how they appear to sensory observation, and these connections can be perceived through spiritual vision.

Thus comments on the Stations of the Cross here follow the account of the spear wound. After first reflecting on one theme, we will therefore now turn to an apparently different one – a phenomenon that the spiritual pupil often encounters – and subsequently will find that this gives us a new basis for understanding the first.

The judgement of Pilate: beginning of the Stations of the Cross

Let us now journey back to the turning point of time, and direct the eyes of our heart to this last, arduous journey of Christ Jesus, starting from the judgement by Pontius Pilate which initiates it.

A leather belt had been tied around the scourged Redeemer, and His shackles were attached to this. Humiliated in this way, yet still standing upright, He was led before the Roman governor. Beside Him, to His right and left, stood the two murderers, sentencing of whom, at the request of the Jewish priests, had been postponed until judgement had been passed on Jesus of Nazareth. They had already been incarcerated for some days. It was the priests' intention to heap greater humiliation on Christ Jesus by having him sentenced and executed alongside these 'impure' ones — as they were called under Jewish law.

Pilate sat on a raised seat before his palace. Behind him lay the temple area. The walls surrounding the temple and its environs bordered directly on the south side of his Jerusalem palace. The judgement seat stood on a wide terrace which formed the main entrance to the palace. A long, semi-circular stairway led up to the terrace. The palace steps stood in a courtyard enclosed by other buildings – including two watchtowers and a colonnade. The latter ended at the forum to the north, and the colonnade sheltered the market. The forum was, at the same time, a thoroughfare for traders and travellers who entered the city through the gates situated in the east wall. Thus every public sentencing could be witnessed directly from the forum, and many people were therefore present when Jesus was condemned, including foreigners not from the city.

The priests and the high council obeyed different laws from those of the Roman empire. This was a law determined by religious traditions which among other things forbade them from approaching too close to the sick, the dead and criminals. For a fairly long time therefore, since occupation by the Romans, a row of dark stones had been positioned near the judgement seat in the ground of the north edge of the square, the forum end, to mark the prescribed 'cleanliness boundary'. Behind this boundary stood the high Jewish officials, communicating with Pilate in a loud voice across the intervening space where the accused were standing.

Pilate's secretary stood behind him. At last, Pilate uttered the sentence of death on Jesus of Nazareth. After the proclamation he himself wrote the judgement, of which the secretary made several copies. Grounds were attached to the sentence, in which Pilate justified his reasons for having Jesus of Nazareth crucified. These grounds were that a religious community with other customs had demanded this verdict of him, and he had ceded to their demand in order to avoid rebellion. The attached grounds for the verdict were read out. Now there followed a storm of protest from the high priests and their followers, because Pilate had thereby placed the responsibility on them, and because the document contained the words 'King of the Jews'. They demanded immediate changes to the grounds for the verdict, to which Pilate did not agree. They also urged that the small board to be attached to the Cross should be reworded from 'King of the Jews' to 'He who claims to be King of the Jews'. But this too was refused. The Gospels report these events with astonishing accuracy.

For the eye of spirit the profound horror of the situation at that time is revealed in its almost unbearable contrasts. The extravagant wealth of the Roman occupiers and the decadence of its representatives on the one hand, and the lordly, unrelenting, bitter Jewish priests on the other stood, in their external cleanliness, facing the humiliated and condemned men. In their midst stood the Christ Light in His unearthly purity.

Pilate himself seemed inwardly shrunk as, surrounded by grandeur, he left the judgement place with the trumpeters preceding him. All the uncertainty of a person without relationship to his cosmic home was concealed behind a façade of pomp and ceremony of the fourth cultural epoch, marked by the decadence of Rome. No doubt he considered himself powerful, but deep within he

Hieronymus Bosch: 'Bearing the Cross' (detail)
Königliches Museum, Ghent

*Matthias Grünewald: 'Crucifixion' (detail), around 1510.
Isenheim Altar, Colmar*

Matthias Grünewald: 'Resurrection' (detail), around 1510.
Isenheim Altar, Colmar

Giacomo Jaquerio: 'Bearing the Cross' (detail), around 1440. San Antonio, Raverso

sensed his impotence in the face of higher powers. The Gospel tells us how Christ draws his attention to this state: 'Thou couldest have no power against me, unless it were given thee from above' (John 19,11). And yet the sentence passed by Pontius Pilate is the decisive moment from which the Mystery of Golgotha began to be fulfilled. Destiny took its course though this verdict. Thus Pilate was in a certain sense the fulfiller of a divine plan.

The verdict for the first time brings into play a cosmic law which Rudolf Steiner described in a somewhat different form when he said that the cultural epochs reflect each other at the midpoint of evolution, the Christ event. As an impetus-giving intervention in Earth evolution, Christ caused reflections between periods and events on earth. This lawfulness already came to mild but perceptible expression during His presence in a human body, in particular in relation to the events unfolding between the judgement and His earthly death. We will examine below what exactly occurred in consequence of the judgement, and how we can understand this reflecting process. But let it be said already that after the sentence was passed, but before death at the Crucifixion, this law was revealed in a prefiguring form, so that each event on the Redeemer's path of suffering led, as though in a mirror image, to another, transformed occurrence at a particular point of the Mystery of Golgotha. Each transformed event was related through this mirroring with what had occurred before.

The sacrificial path

Through transformation of preceding events it was also the case that the unspeakable torments and humiliations which the Son of Man had to suffer in his earthly powerlessness were not followed by hatred and despair but, despite continually increasing agonies, by the growth of ever more love and confidence. Deprived of all human dignity and in the greatest state of wretchedness He stood there as the wood for the Cross was being fetched — He, God Himself — but at the same time radiant with spiritual glory. For supersensible perception this glory of God was and is overpowering, precisely at those moments of outer powerlessness. This is the triumph of truth's beauty.

It was as if the hierarchies had poured out all their treasures over their King. And so He, Christ Jesus, trod the path that He was willing to tread for the sake of humanity.

The priests had achieved what they had long intended — but only outwardly. They had forced Him into silence and brought His work among human beings to a premature end. They had brought about His physical death. And now, after the judgement, they ran to their empty idolatry in the temple, which had wholly lost its justification when Jesus was sentenced. They ran into an empty, desolate building, away from the temple of their future. It was a ghastly, paradoxical coincidence that on this day of preparation for the feast of Pesach the slaughter of lambs began and all the priests streamed to the temple, while the true Redeemer

Lamb had to embark on his arduous sacrificial path. After the judgement, most of the priests returned to these animals, the ritual, pre-Christian 'representatives' of the true Lamb. In pre-Christian times, such animals were an expression of ritual sacrifice to the Logos still dwelling in the cosmos. But now the Logos was on earth, was with them, but they ran to the temple where lambs were being slaughtered and away from the One to whom they meant to offer their sacrifice.

Like a poignant metaphor the external course of events and inner truth contrasted utterly at these moments: on the one hand the bringer of love and truth, despised, condemned, slandered – the Christ made ritually unclean through contact with the criminals, outwardly defiled and broken, yet inwardly radiantly pure, the representative of love; and on the other hand, the high priests, outwardly kosher and unsullied, in their wafting, perfumed clothes, in expensive sandals, walking to the temple, yet inwardly besmirched by the raging of adversary powers within them, whose paths they were pursuing.

The procession that began moving from the forum towards Golgotha was the greatest indignity that the world ever suffered. Yet despite its horror and cruelty it appeared like a truly royal train: in front came the trumpeters announcing the Crucifixion so as to clear a way through the city. They were followed by the hard-bitten mercenaries of the Roman army who bore tools for the Crucifixion: hammers, nails, ropes, tall, narrow ladders, and also instruments of torture. These men also bore the main uprights for the crosses for the two murderers. Behind them ran a boy bearing the board with the words, in three languages, *Jesus of Nazareth, King of the Jews,* and on a stick the crown of thorns woven like a king's cap — not a kind of wreath as often depicted.

Then the Redeemer Himself followed, the leather belt around his waist with broad, iron lugs through which ran the four ropes by means of which four mercenaries pulled and tugged Him, either forwards, backwards or to the side. Directly behind Him walked two other mercenaries, guiding the wood of the Cross which He bore upon His

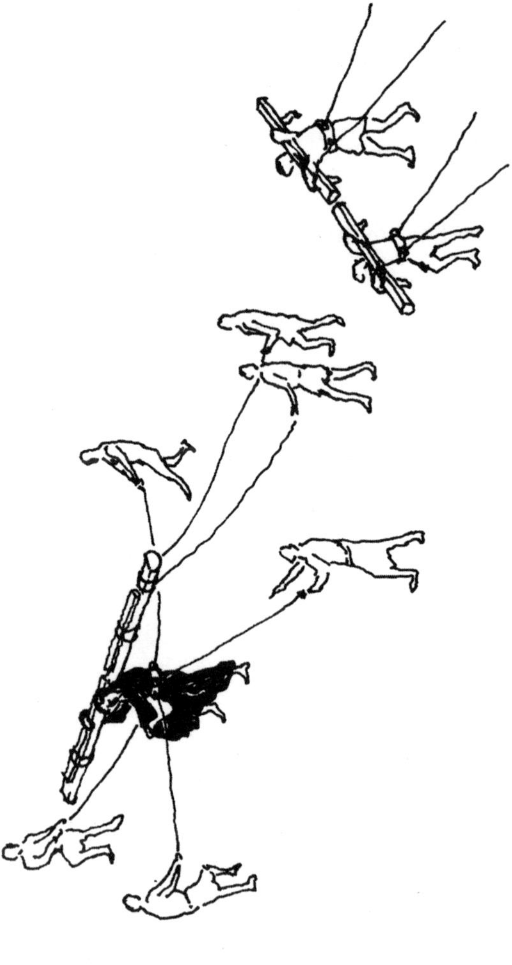

Carrying the Cross

shoulder. The Lord did not bear the Cross in the way it is traditionally portrayed in art, for the wood had not yet been put together into a cross: this was only done at Golgotha. Thus the two shorter, rectangular crosspieces were tied lengthwise one behind each other on top of the heavy main upright. The Lord bore this burden on His right shoulder, placing His right arm over it. With His left hand – when possible – He supported the beams, but mostly, so as not to fall, He had to use His left hand to raise the woollen over-garment He wore. This had grown long and heavy. After the scourging it was returned to Him, but saturated with foul-smelling fluid to mock Him.

Alongside the Redeemer marched a column of Roman soldiers with spears and rattling, metal shin-armour. Behind Him came the two felons, their arms tied over the crosspieces of their crosses, and each likewise held on ropes by mercenaries. At the rear came around 15 Pharisees on asses. Sometimes, when the procession halted for a moment, these separated and rode up and down, or went to the head of the procession.

The seven falls

The Lord first had to be led through narrow streets
because the main streets were thronging with many
people who had come from outside the city for the
festival preparations and were heading for the
temple square. Jerusalem was also, at that time, the
sacred place of all Jews, who therefore flocked there
at feast-days from all provinces of the empire.

The first fall

When the procession reached the first crossroads
and began to turn down a street running south-
wards, the Redeemer fell for the first time. In Jerusalem at this time there was no proper waste-water
system as yet, and open drainage channels therefore
ran through most of the streets, crossing wherever
two roads intersected. In the middle of these crossing channels a raised stone was always placed, to
help people get across. The Redeemer, with the
heavy weight on His shoulders, was unable to
manage the leap on to this crossing stone. He stop-
ped for a moment. But he was mercilessly tugged

and pulled onwards, causing Him to lose His balance and fall into the drainage channel.*

The Pharisees rode forward at this point, mocking and asking with scornful undertone whether the

---

*Based on my experience from several lecture occasions, it seems to me necessary to add a personal remark here which is only of significance for anyone who feels addressed by it. Some readers may find it unpalatable to imagine the Son of God in such a humiliating situation as this account may require them to. It belongs, surely, to a schooling of broad-mindedness to be able to accompany in one's thoughts not only the lofty moments of Christ's incarnation but also the most degrading ones. Any one who has ever experienced – in his soul or in a rudimentary way upon his own body – how the beloved Redeemer sacrificed all His powers for humanity, will never wish to turn away and leave Him alone in His indescribable suffering in order to spare his own sensitivities. What, apart from our faith and Christian deeds, can we do for the Christ being other than at least participate in what was inflicted on Him by our own human race? How could we turn away? He suffered so greatly to endow us with the potential for freedom, and we find it too difficult to contemplate His suffering? People often refuse to believe in anything that unsettles the basis of their safe view of the world, even though it is beyond dispute. Those who establish a view of the world that prevents it ever disturbing them, will not develop insight or knowledge. Knowledge is not merely given. It arises only in the earthly vale of incarnation, through love and suffering.

(Contd)

King required help to rise again. A few mercenaries came running and beat Christ Jesus with fists.

The crown of thorns was also placed on His head once more, and some of the mercenaries took the stick from the hand of the boy who had been carrying the crown and beat Him around the head with it, to drive the thorns deep into His forehead. Then they loaded the heavy beams on His right shoulder again and the procession continued, turning to the left and heading for the higher slopes (see drawing on page 101).

The second fall

The procession approached a high wall on the left-hand side, which enclosed a large complex of

---

(Contd from previous page)

One insight which we can acquire from Christ's path of suffering is that the outer humiliations, the powerlessness, were a part of His sacrifice: that is, a penetration of the deepest point of human incarnation. Light can only shine for us when we are in darkness. The sacrifice of powerlessness is a great mystery of the Christ event, and is vastly more lofty than any all-too-human sensitivities. Nevertheless, I would like to assure readers that I have here refrained from mentioning the most drastic occurrences on the Stations of the Cross, giving only a vague idea of what is most essential for understanding the historical circumstances.

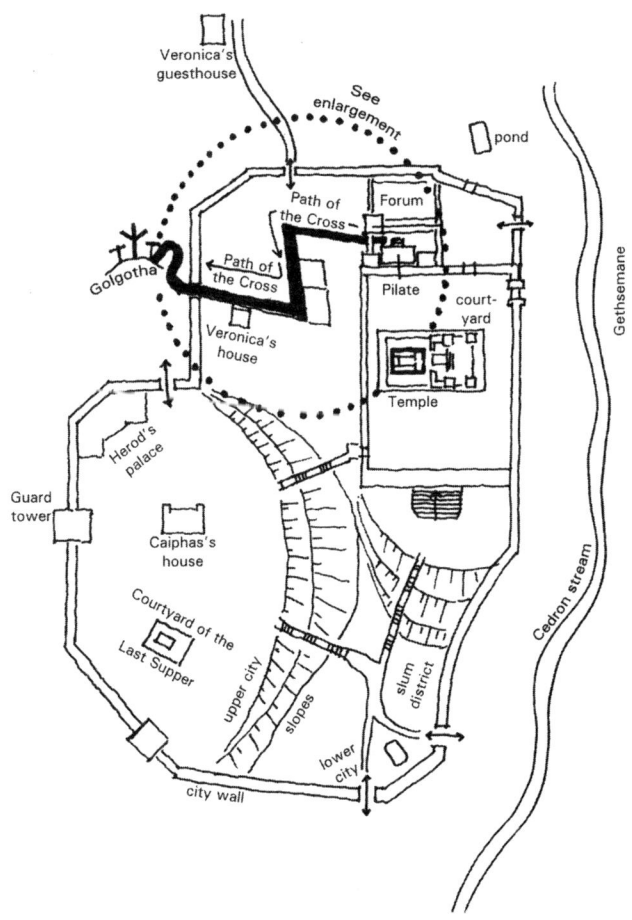

Jerusalem at the time of Christ

buildings. Several courtyards formed a way through
this complex, through which one could take a short-
cut when coming from Zion and heading for the
temple or the forum. One of the gates of these
buildings led towards the now broader street, on
which the procession was advancing (see drawing).
John – the disciple whom the Lord loved – and the
women came to this gate by the short-cut, to meet
the Master on his way and do what they could to
offer him support. With John were the mother of
Jesus, Mary Magdalene, the mother of Jacob, Martha
and Maria Salome. As the procession neared this
gateway, the Lord first saw the mother of Jesus, and
John. As if the sight of His loved ones had struck
Him to the core – because life had tasted so sweet
when they were still able to be together, and now
community with His faithful must end – He collapsed. The mother tore herself free from the arm of
the disciple and ran towards the Son as He fell to His
knees. She touched His cheek where the blood was
running down from wounds caused by the pressure
of the thorns. For an instant everything came to a
standstill, and some of the Roman soldiers, through

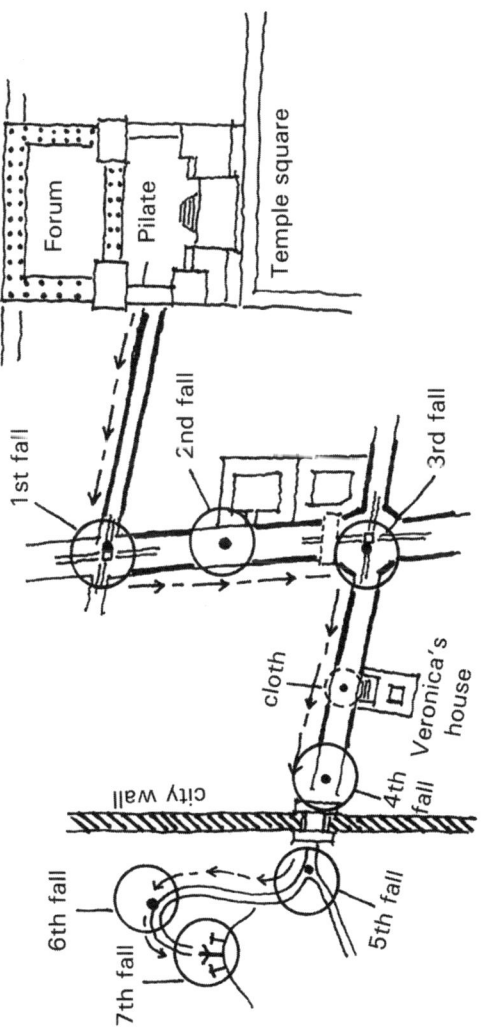

The Path of the Cross

whose midst the mother had forced her way, were inwardly moved by this moment.

But this meeting did not last long, for the soldiers were directed to lead the mother away. John quickly joined her and prevented them taking hold of her too roughly. He led her back to the gateway, where she sat down on a cornerstone. The Lord took up the beams again and the procession began to move forward.

The third fall

Soon they reached another, square-like crossroads, shortly before a large, stone gate arch (see drawing). And again, there was a crossing stone where the Lord once more fell. He tried to break His fall with the left hand, but He fell on His knees, and had to use His right hand also, so as not to be too severely injured – at which the wooden beams fell to the ground beside Him. As people tried to drag him upright again by tugging on the rope attached to his belt, all the while slandering and threatening Him, He was so weak and faint – also because of the hours of interrogation and the unspeakably cruel torture inflicted on Him throughout the previous night and the early hours of the morning – that He could hardly get up again, or even stand upright.

The Pharisees were worried that He might die there and then. For this reason they directed the soldiers to find someone to help Christ carry the wooden beams. This was not done out of any concern for His well being, but they wanted at all costs to ensure His public humiliation on the Cross.

At the place of the third fall many well-attired Jews were passing on their way to the temple. However, none of them could be commandeered for such a task. Some showed sympathy, as one could read in their faces, while others were afraid to be contaminated. These anxieties were the consequence of the wholly excessive laws imposed by the Pharisees, whose name was very apt: the word, *pharush* in Aramaic meant someone who was 'sequestered' or kept apart. The Pherisarot (Pharisees) expounded an extreme doctrine of cleanliness which related primarily to one's external mode of life rather than the inner soul. They wished to impose on all the Jewish people the comprehensive, traditional command of cleanliness which in the past had been applied only to the priest caste. They tried to prevent any resistance to such demands by spreading the rumour that the Messiah would never otherwise appear.

Here again we have the sharpest contrast between reality and the sensory world of appearances: the Messiah whom they hoped for stood before them and, quite at odds with their decadent ideas of cleanliness, was besmirched and defiled. Here, like a thunderous sign, the world of spirit was telling them that the kingdom of God is not of this world, and that it was their task to perceive true, inward purity of the soul. But they remained blind to all such signs.

Finally, accompanied by his sons, a Jew came along who, to judge by his clothes, was of low birth (and might not have been a Jew at all). On festival days he cultivated the gardens of Jerusalem outside the city bounds, and was carrying timber on his shoulder to sell in the forum. We know his name, Simon of Cyrene. He was dragged to the place where Christ lay, and sharply threatened when he tried to refuse to help. The compulsion and personal humiliation were offensive to him. Simon was ordered to help Christ up, which he did full of disgust, for he did not want to sully himself with the unclean and blood-soaked garments of the Lord. Initially he had the feeling that none of this concerned him, not yet knowing that this would actually be the most significant moment of all his earthly incarnations. The load was now distributed between the Redeemer, who walked in front, and on Simon, who grasped hold of one of the crossbeams and the upright. In this way they went a little further uphill, until the procession turned off to the West.

Veronica's cloth

From there they went perhaps 80 metres. Although it was not a great distance from the forum to the city gate leading to Golgotha, it was a long, arduous journey, for every step was an endlessly heavy burden. We cannot avoid a sense that the Stations of the Cross could only be accomplished with the help of the angels. Soon the procession approached the house of the woman whose name tradition tells us was Veronica (which means 'the true countenance'). In fact her name was different. She was prosperous, married and a respected woman.

When one passed out of the city through the north gate, a quarter of an hour's journey along the main road brought one to an inn which belonged to her. There she had often served Christ, His disciples and friends and the women, and given them accommodation for the night. Her family was one that longed for the Messiah, and may have had connections with the Essenes. She was most likely very closely acquainted with or maybe even related to the family of John the Baptist; for when the latter's earthly remains were buried she wore, as was customary for relatives of the dead, a special over-garment with a great tear over the breast, as a sign of mourning. I estimate that she was around 60 years old at the time of the Crucifixion.

Like all the women close to Christ she wanted to do whatever she could to help to make His sufferings more tolerable, and to show Him her deep reverence. None of those whose love for the Master had been kindled could do anything to prevent the destiny that now awaited Him, which seemed to be taking its inexorable course. There was really nothing more to be done than what occurred to this woman. She wanted to offer Him a fine drink, at the same time passing Him a handkerchief, as was the Jewish tradition. Offering a handkerchief, to wipe away sweat or tears, was a specifically Jewish tradition of those times. Giving a cloth to travellers, mourners or exhausted people to whom one wished to show respect, and with which they could dry their face, was a common custom. Such forms of respect towards one's fellow men also included foot washing and anointing. At a time when many paths and roads passed through empty, lonely areas, and the summer was long, hot and dusty, it was a natural thing for a host to offer his guests a special bowl for washing the feet. And if friends arrived, the host would himself wash their feet as a sign of his friendship. Anointing was the highest form of respect at the time of Christ. Such unctions, as they were called, consisted either of a good oil combined with rare flower perfumes, or of precious, thicker, milky or clear extracts of oriental plant juices and fruits. Anointing was originally reserved for kings, but also came to be used as last unction at burials, or at birth.

Courageously Veronica rushed out of her house, which bordered directly on the street on which the procession was approaching (see drawing). She ran down the steps to the street and without hesitating pushed her way through the crowd and the soldiers. The procession came to a halt. She had veiled her head under an over-garment, and over her right shoulder she bore a thin, bright throw of cloth – the most precious material she owned – the bottom end of which she offered to the Redeemer, at the same time briefly bending her knee to Him in devotion. He gladly accepted her loving gift. Continuing to grasp the wood of the cross with the right arm, He took the end of the cloth in His free left hand and pressed His face into it. I saw how, because of the bloody impression His face left on the cloth, He even tried to fold the cloth again with the right hand laid over the wooden beams, as if it was unpleasant to Him to have dirtied the precious cloth; yet this action was imbued with so much wisdom and rightness that this impression could no doubt only arise through his overwhelming humility. He handed the cloth to her again full of gratitude. He took nothing of the drink, for the soldiers prevented it.* The Pharisees were beside themselves because the Messiah, whom they wished to brand as an impostor, had been publicly revered by this act. They gave orders for Him to be beaten once again. In the meantime Simon had entirely changed: a sense had taken hold of him that an unsullied, sacred inwardness dwelt in this defiled and humiliated

---

* From a higher perspective the soldiers' intervention here can be seen as part of a divine plan, for the drink contained fermented plant juices and, because of its alcohol content, could not be drunk by Christ Jesus, since it would have dulled the I forces.

man. It seemed to him that he was walking in the footprints of a king, and he was completely filled with reverence and emotion.

The fourth fall

Shortly before passing through the city walls by the deep west gate that led towards Golgotha, Christ fell for the fourth time (see drawing). The middle of the road directly in front of the gate passage contained a large depression in the ground, like a giant pothole, filled with waste water. Simon, behind Him, shifted over to the right as he saw it coming. This redistributed the weight of the beams, and the Lord fell into the deep puddle. The heavy wood collapsed on top of Him and ended up piled on His back, for Simon too had lost his balance when the Lord fell – a profound metaphor. As I remember it, Christ spoke a psalm of the Prophets that was fulfilled with this fall, at which He was beaten once more, including with a cudgel. Simon was horrified at the soldiers' cruelty and the nearly hysterical curses of the Pharisees, and put his own life at risk with a loud, courageous protest at these actions. He himself received a violent stroke, and the command to be silent. The two mercenaries walking behind the Christ, who held the cords fastened to Jesus' belt, ran forwards to the two in front, and together they pulled Him up again, with the wood on His back. It was an unspeakably cruel and mortifying scene.

The fifth fall

Just outside the gate, at a fork in the road on the way to the Golgotha hill, there came towards Him a larger group of mourning women, who likewise stretched out cloths to Him. At the sight of them He again collapsed and became faint. His strength was increasingly deserting Him. When He came to His senses once more, and Simon, full of compassion and reverence, helped Him stand, He comforted these women with a few words: they should, He said, use the handkerchiefs themselves to wipe away their own tears, and care for their children. Those were His approximate words. But these words suggested to me a quite different meaning than one would ascribe to them today. They were spoken like a metaphor or parable, formulated in the style of those times but nevertheless deep as a lake, like a significant message of truth to the future. We can be sure that when He spoke of 'children' He meant something other, something more. What is contained in the word 'child' is, after all, something of future potential that has not yet grown to fullness; something still in the process of developing and growing. In His words lay a benevolent exhortation and a prophecy: the children of tomorrow were, at that moment, the crying women themselves. He was admonishing them to think of their future. If they were crying at that moment, His words seemed to suggest, it was a good sign. And He added wordlessly, and yet experienced as a reverberation in the souls of those present:

> *The tears you are now shedding will in future make you thirst for me, and I will thirst for the tears of your children.*

He had thus addressed the inmost soul of these mourning women and of all those present; and the metaphor of children, by which was meant their own future being and potential, left in them an inkling of human responsibility towards the world of spirit, working on into the furthest future with every deed and action. Something like a feeling of truth in relation to the Christian mystery of karma rose in them in an instant through His words.

The sixth fall

As the path to Golgotha turned back on itself in a U-shaped loop (see drawing), the Lord suddenly halted. He saw the end of His path before Him. His gaze, which seemed to be without beginning or end, showed Him a picture of His further destiny, which would impose on Him the most arduous of all sacrifices. As He looked towards the pale sun, the solar rays and the gaze of the Christ Sun met at the summit of the Crucifixion hill. This was the last place on earth which He would walk upon in a physical body: the place where the Sun would enter the earth. Again He collapsed, the wooden beams cutting into His shoulder. He was brutally pulled to His feet, and He now stood unsteadily.

A strange mood held sway. The more powerless and faint the Redeemer became, the greater grew His glory, love and forgiveness towards His tormentors –

which drove them all the wilder. They sensed that they could not destroy Him, nor break His will. Never before, with someone condemned to death, had the Pharisees, mercenaries and soldiers experienced anything like what was happening now. They sensed that this man did not collapse inwardly, that whatever inhuman things were done to Him He did not complain nor curse; that, on the contrary, He seemed to endure his fate with ever more willingness. His dreadful physical state could not hide the glory of His inner steadfastness. But they could not grasp why this was so. They did not know that He could see His spiritual home behind death. He knew what they did not. And the dull sense of this fact drove them to the worst excesses against Him.

From the place where the Lord fell one had to climb very steeply to the top. The ground was of loose, slippery rocks so that one could barely keep one's grip. Simon tried to protest again at the mercilessness of the tormentors who were dragging the Lord up the hill, but his position behind Christ meant that much of the load shifted onto his shoulders during the climb, and he had enough to do not to lose his footing and drop the beams.

The seventh fall

The seventh fall, on the Crucifixion hill, was the last. The Lord finally collapsed under the wood and did not pick it up again. He was bathed in sweat and His senses were failing. The wooden beams were untied as, under the urging cries of the executors, He slowly began to raise Himself again. Hardly had He got to His feet when He was dragged back to the ground, to be stretched upon the Cross which had now been put together, and to measure and mark the nail points. Simon wanted to stay with Him, but he was driven away, back down the hill, into the crowd of watchers and attendants.

The seven words on the Cross

Here I wish to interrupt description of the historical events with a reflection on the spiritual context connected with them.

I spoke previously of 'reflections' between events from the passing of sentence to the Lord's death. Seven falls occur up to the point where He is nailed to the Cross, and it is not by chance that in the hours between the nailing and death, seven most significant sayings are spoken, as tradition has preserved to this day. However, discussion of these seven words from the Cross and the circumstances under which they were spoken must be preceded by emphasizing that the Redeemer in fact spoke far more than these seven words. He had to suffer on the Cross for around three hours before death occurred. Everything he spoke was religious in nature, drawn from the sayings of the Prophets, and was instantaneously fulfilled as He spoke it, as all prophecies had been focused upon Him. These sayings of the Prophets could be recognized by the fact that they were often spoken in Hebrew, whereas the Lord otherwise spoke Aramaic. Sometimes only His lips moved, perhaps in pain, like a whimper, but perhaps also forming words that I was unable to understand.

I do not intend to detail all the events of the Crucifixion, but only to say something about the words from the Cross, relating these to the cosmic rhythms already mentioned previously. The seven falls do indeed come to spiritual utterance in the seven words from the Cross, in a kind of 'parallel reflection'. The moment of nailing forms the 'mirror' point, a nodal point for the inner transformation of each of the falls. The seven words contain, in transmuted form, the impulses which accompanied the seven falls. To be able to grasp these (spiritual) connections, it was necessary first to present the observations on the spear-wound mystery.

The sketch below aims to give a clear picture of how, through its transformation by the Christ being, the first fall resurfaces in changed form in the inner content of the first word. Similarly, a correspon-

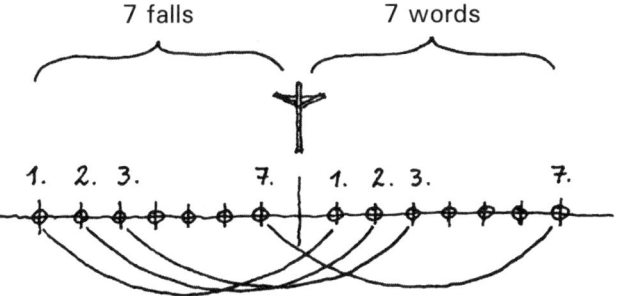

dence can be shown between the second fall and the second word.

Based on this correspondence I now want to outline the seven words from the Cross in brief pictures:

The first word

After Jesus was tied and nailed to the Cross and it was erected, and the two criminals were also crucified (in their case with tight cords), the soldiers, and the Pharisees still more, began to mock and jeer at that terrible sight. But the murderer also, crucified to the left of Jesus, whose Cross was turned away from the sun, started cursing and joining in the mockery of the Pharisees about the Redeemer.

In this scene, too, external circumstances manifested the spiritual background to what was happening. The Cross on which the Saviour hung was turned so that His gaze travelled westwards, or, to be more precise, north-west. The somewhat lower, T-shaped crosses of the murderers were at a slightly oblique angle to the Lord's Y-shaped Cross. In other words, all three crosses stood on the base, as it were, of an open triangle. The mocking murderer to the left of the Lord was facing north-east, turned wholly away from the sun, while his brother on the right of the Lord looked towards the midday sun. He was therefore gazing at the sun's embodiment, for he was turned towards the sun rays which seemed to shine through Christ.

This new humiliation and mockery lasted for about half an hour, and then the soldiers who had guarded the procession of condemned on the way to Golgotha, and supervised the nailing and erection of the Cross, marched off with calls of mockery, to be replaced at the 'place of the skull' by around 50 other soldiers under the leadership of the Arabic first officer named Abn Adar. The Pharisees continued their fury unabated, deriving an appalling enjoyment from seeing the Lord helpless on the Cross. They called out the worst insults, saying that Christ Jesus was a liar, and cited His prophecy that the temple would be rebuilt within three days as supposed proof of His purely human origins. The temple was still standing in its place, they said, none of them grasping the real meaning of these prophetic words.

The Redeemer then spoke these words to them (Luke 23,24):

Father, forgive them, for they know not what they do.

Here the mockery at the first fall — for there too the Pharisees had mocked His kingdom — was transformed into a plea to the Father for their forgiveness.

But if we quote these words of the Lord today we should nevertheless be aware that times have changed and that the same conditions no longer apply as at the time of the Crucifixion. Nowadays people ought to know what they are doing. We stand at an evolutionary point where Lucifer's temptations have already been constrained by Christ's deed, and Ahriman has already been laid in chains. Of course this does not mean that after this deed the world's cruelty has diminished; but, in relation to the free development of the consciousness soul in the human being, the influence of Ahriman and Lucifer was confined and limited by the sacrifice of Christ. If today, despite our awakened consciousness, we turn to these powers and then expect forgiveness, we can no longer appeal to the fact that we do not know what we are doing. Such a stance nurtures Sorat impulses* in contemporary life. The human being then behaves as though the Christ sacrifice and all subsequent evolutionary processes were non-existent.

The second word

The sky darkened and the first signs of changes in nature became evident. An eerie mood prevailed. The Pharisees had fallen silent and all gazed towards the sky. The soldiers and mercenaries retreated from the Cross and withdrew some distance from the hill of Golgotha. Now the moment had come when the Lord's loved ones could approach the Cross. The mother and the disciple whom the Lord loved stood directly before it, and behind these were Maria Cleophas (the daughter of the eldest sister of Jesus' mother) and Mary Magdalene.

As these four stood before Him, Christ uttered the

---

* According to Rudolf Steiner, the strongest power of evil. Sorat is an arch-enemy of the human I or ego. (Editor's note.)

second word, inaugurating soul relationship so as to lead blood relationship towards its end. He said to the mother:

Woman, behold your son.

And to John:

Behold your mother.

In these words (John 19,26 f.) we can find the transformation of the second fall, when the mother and John both approached Him. They became related to each other in a quite new sense through being related in their Christ-seeking souls. True relatedness amongst people in future involves pursuing this same path: the path towards the Christ being that passes through the gate of Christ and bears us back towards the Father.

The third word

The tumult of the crowd as the skies darkened did not calm. But the murderer to the left continued — almost unshaken by the darkening heavens — to urge the Redeemer to descend from the Cross, in a shrill, mocking voice. As he uttered these insults, the soul of the murderer to the right was wholly transformed.

He had witnessed the Christian legacy to the world of the new relationship amongst human beings. And although the contortions of his limbs and the ropes that bound him made him suffer as terribly as his scornful, cursing brother, he recognized the Son of God in Jishoa, in the human being Jesus of Nazareth, and begged Him to ask His Father for mercy for him. At that Christ said to him (Luke 23,43):

> Verily I say unto thee, this day thou wilt be with me in paradise.

The third fall led to the destined encounter with Simon of Cyrene. Like the murderer on the right hand of Christ who only perceived and acknowledged Christ as he was being crucified, Simon only turned inwardly to Christ *after* picking up the Cross. It is only through suffering, through our own involvement and entanglement in the threads of destiny, that we develop the capacity to gain knowledge and insight. If, despite or because of such situations, we turn to the world of spirit, we may pass through the gateway into the world beyond, and are accepted there in love.

A wonderful providence may also be mentioned here: the conditions which led to this third word from the Cross arose from direct realization of His legacy to humanity, as expressed shortly before in the second word. We can scarcely imagine a clearer expression of this new gift to humanity than the decision by the man crucified to the right of Christ to separate himself from his blood brother, so as to unite with Christ. Thus the earlier saying of Christ was fulfilled: 'Whoever does not deny wife and child, father and mother, brother and sister, cannot be my disciple!' (Luke 14,26, in Rudolf Steiner's translation*).

The fourth word
Some time passed and then the earth suddenly began to quake. Panic and chaos broke out every-

---

*In his lecture of 22 May 1908, in *The Gospel of St John* (Anthroposophic Press 1962).

where – not just outside the city gates but above all in the temple and amongst the priests. Pilate was being blamed for having caused these natural phenomena through his sentencing of Jesus of Nazareth.

Some Pharisees now professed their faith in Christ Jesus. Anxious calls and loud wailing could be heard everywhere. Many people ran away from Golgotha, back to their homes in the city. Others ran out of the city towards Golgotha to see with their own eyes the reason for what they supposed to be the end of the world. At this, Pilate sent hundreds of soldiers to Golgotha and ordered the city gates to be shut.

The officer Abn Adar forbade mockery of the Lord.

The Redeemer's pains increased, His breath grew ever heavier and slower because of the severe constriction of his chest by the fetters. As he spoke again He saw death before Him (Matthew 27,46; Mark 15,34):

Eli, Eli, lama sabachthani

I have mentioned previously that these words contain a dual meaning.* Since the physical events were a reflection of the supersensible, everything that occurred during the Mystery of Golgotha had a double significance. During Christ's descent to hell, also, the phenomenon of dual meaning or the correspondence between two events is discernible: the deeper Christ descended into the abyss, the higher, simultaneously, was his ascent, and the more the conditions for His ascent were created.

When the Lord spoke the fourth word, His physical life forces were almost completely exhausted — a sight at which one's heart breaks. Yet for the eye of spirit He shone out like a victor as death approached, as brightly as at the transfiguration on Mount Tabor. These two manifestations were wholly opposed. And thus His words resounded from the physical world on the one hand, out of the physical organism that was passing over into the death process:

---

* See lecture of 12 December 2004 in the book *And If He Has Not Been Raised*...

My God, my God, why hast thou forsaken me?

Yet on the other hand these words resonated from the mouth of the Son of Man preparing for His true birth, shortly to recreate and renew the primal archetype of humanity:

My God, my God, how hast thou elevated me!

The correspondence to this fourth word, that is, the fourth fall, must also include the encounter with Veronica which occurred shortly before that fall. The compassion and reverence shown in the offering of the cloth, *elevated* the Lord in His abject state in the eyes of all the people. All those present bore witness to this and felt it in their hearts. Outwardly defiled, He shone out in inner glory.

The fifth word

Shortly before His path of suffering ended, around ten minutes before death occurred, He said:

I thirst!

John had to tell Him that they had forgotten to offer Him some of what they had brought with them.

Mary Magdalene, particularly, could not forgive herself for this. It also seemed to hurt the Lord that He had been forgotten in His thirst. They could have given Him something to drink during all the commotion. But these are not the deeper reasons for his loved ones failing to give him drink, nor why He spoke these two words. The drinks they had brought with them all contained a small amount of alcohol, which could not, under any circumstances, be given to the body of Jesus. Alcohol dulls and numbs the I. Since humanity's I was about to come to birth, such a drink could not be administered. Instead, Abn Adar passed up a pole with a cloth dipped in vinegar to His mouth, from which He did indeed refresh Himself. It may strike us as strange that the Redeemer gladly took such a bitter drink, but the reason for this will become clear in the course of our account.

However, the Lord did not utter the fifth word, 'I thirst' (John 19,29) solely on account of physical thirst. In this thirst of the Lord we find a reflection of the fifth fall before the women at the city gate, who were urged not to forget the Redeemer in future:

they were to thirst for Him, and He would thirst for their devotion. The world of spirit lives from humanity's thirst for truth and love, and for the spiritual world itself!

The sixth word

And Christ said (John 19,30):

It is finished.

This was spoken as fulfilment of His arduous journey, and represents the parallel to His sixth fall that occurred when Golgotha and the end of His path of suffering came into view.

The seventh word

At the moment of death, almost inaudibly, the seventh word (Luke 23,46) passed His lips:

Father, into thy hands I commend my spirit.

This saying corresponds to the seventh fall that took place on Golgotha itself, when He fainted for a few moments, after which He did not pick up the wood of the Cross again. Just as the Stations of the Cross ended with the seventh fall, so with the seventh word Christ's incarnation on earth came to an end.

Thus we see the parallel correspondences of spiritual impulses in the transformation of the seven falls into the Lord's seven words from the Cross. We can observe two phenomena here: firstly, a parallelism, and secondly a mirroring effect. The parallels arise between the falls and the sacred words, the first fall transforming into the first word, and the second fall into the second word etc. The mirroring, with its nodal point at the nailing of Christ to the Cross, relates to the transformed content of the words from the Cross (see drawing on page 119).

Transformation of the fallen blood

In relation to the seven falls and the seven words from the Cross I would now like to give some deeper spiritual-scientific insights that reveal a quite different kind of mirroring.

Christ was nailed to the Cross on Golgotha because – as Rudolf Steiner describes this in various ways — He, as representative of humanity, allowed the unpurified 'egotistical blood'* to flow out of the physical organization. Behind this reality stands one of the mysteries of the Stations of the Cross and the flowing of Christ's blood at the Crucifixion.

We know from Rudolf Steiner that there were *two* Jesus children, the so-called Solomon child and the Nathan child of the Luke Gospel.† This is also, in fact, one of the most vital discoveries in relation to the Mystery of Golgotha! The Solomon Jesus child bore in himself the I of Zarathustra. At the age of 12 the soul and the I of the Solomon child had matured to such an extent that he could lay aside his body and enter the pure, intact body of the Luke child; then, at the age of 30, he departed from this body again when the Logos entered it at the Jordan baptism.

This Zarathustra I was basically a profoundly mature earthly I, so highly developed that the laws

---

* See the lecture of 25 March 1908 in *The Gospel of St John* (Anthroposophic Press 1962).
† See Rudolf Steiner, *The Spiritual Guidance of the Individual and Humanity* (Anthroposophic Press 1992).

of the normal rhythm of incarnation no longer applied to it. The Zarathustra individuality belongs to the so-called 24 'Elders' described by John in his Apocalypse. He is a kind of impulse spirit who, together with 23 other such spirits, enhances the destiny of earthly and human evolution. Just as a day has 24 hours, so the whole period of planetary evolution passing through seven planetary stages has 24 impetus-giving spirits of humanity. However, we should not imagine that the many hundreds of thousands of years of our embodiment can be sub-divided into 24 equal periods like the hours in a day, and accord each of these equal periods to an Elder. In this case time plays a subordinate role. Human evolutionary impulses are not necessarily tied to a fixed schema but correspond to earth and human evolution. Just as one can cut a cake into slices of different sizes, so the influence and working of the 24 Elders seated by God's throne vary in their effect on earthly periods of time. These 24 Elders incarnate in their true impetus-giving mission in *one* — we could call it 'chief' — incarnation. Three very well known Elder spirits were Zarathustra, Moses and Elijah. Now it might be objected that Zara-thustra, Moses and Elijah incarnated very closely together, compared to the many thousands of years of our Earth evolution. In a different context* I previously developed the following sketch:

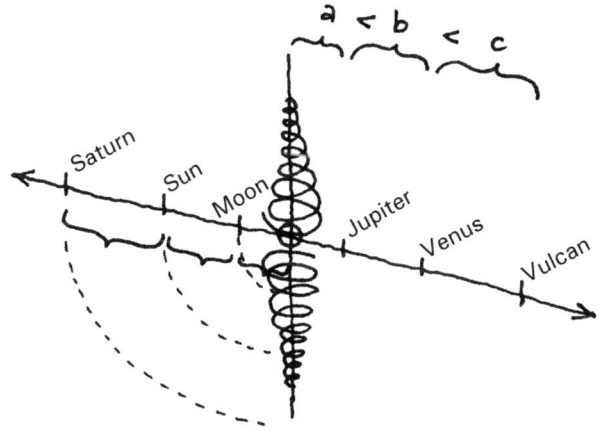

Drawing on this schema I described the path of the Redeemer through the depths of the earth during His descent to the abyss, which made pos-sible a simultaneous ascent of the resurrection body of Christ (see lower and upper spirals). The seven

* In the lecture dated 30 January 2004, in my book *And If He Has Not Been Raised...*

planetary embodiments on the lengthways axis
show that in passing through the depths of the earth
the Christ spirit also penetrates the earth as total
organism in its comprehensive evolution, as it were
passing through past, present and future conditions
of the earth. If we now return to the question of why
three of the 24 Elders, Zarathustra, Moses and Elijah, incorporated their impulses into humanity over
a relatively short successive period, the above sketch
can help. It is striking that the planetary conditions
of Moon and Jupiter lie much closer to the focal or
crown point, the Mystery of Golgotha, than do the
planetary conditions of Moon and Sun to each other,
or Jupiter and Venus. This is because the density of
evolutionary potential is greatest in proximity to the
Christ intervention. This is similar to the way a
water vortex speeds up everything lying in
immediate proximity to its core, compared to what
lies further away from it.

In Zarathustra, Moses and Elijah we have three
successive leaders of humanity who prepare the Sun
mystery. At the time of the birth of the Solomon
Jesus, Zarathustra had already given his impulse to

the world, and his incarnation as the Solomon Jesus child should not be seen as a normal consecutive incarnation. This spiritual being acquired a special role by creating the conditions necessary to allow worldly wisdom — which can only develop at all by encountering hindrances such as ahrimanic and luciferic temptation — to stream into a body that was *free* of these luciferic and ahrimanic influences. Thus, when he was twelve, the wisdom of the Solomon Jesus child flowed into the body of the intact, unsullied Luke child and continued to form this body until the point when the Logos descended at the baptism. It was only this pure body of the St Luke Jesus, to the largest possible extent unsullied by the influence of the adversarial powers, that could provide a dwelling place for the Logos on earth. This unsullied boy was, accordingly, born to a different mother than the Solomon child — who did not stand at the foot of the Cross in her own physical body, since she had died previously. This mother of the Luke child may also be called the *virginal* Mary. The Jesus body hanging on the Cross was the Luke Jesus body, the intact and inviolate one.

Once we have grasped all this, a profound question arises. How can 'luciferic' blood flow out of Christ's wounds from the intact Luke body, on behalf of all humanity, if this body was unsullied by the luciferic influence? The 'new dweller' in this body – the Christ Spirit Himself – had, after all, also overcome the temptations of Lucifer in the desert. How did impure blood enter this wholly pure body?

We should not pass over such questions or details too easily, since they lead us to the true secrets of human evolution. Through conscientious preoccupation with such questions, which may initially appear insoluble, we can eventually come to fundamental insights. Let me here encourage everyone to pursue the questions they have in relation to a spiritual phenomenon, for only by doing so will they find the answers...

Let us recall the Lord's last night on the Mount of Olives. The 'sweated blood' which comes from Christ Jesus is not only due to expectation of the pain and suffering awaiting Him on His last journey, but from a vision of the whole weight of sin that He will have to bear for humanity. At the moment He is sentenced, Jesus Christ's path of sacrifice is unalterably sealed.

This is roughly comparable with the following phenomenon: the human spirit beyond the threshold undertakes quite particular things for a forthcoming life. Immediately before its next incarnation, before conception, it has a pre-vision of these intentions. As the spirit incarnates this life-plan is forgotten initially. But at some point in our lives we come to a time where we must put this plan into practice. Then, usually, realizing it proves less self-evident that the soul perceived it to be before birth.

Thus, before His descent into the Jesus body, the Logos had made His aim self-sacrifice out of endless love for the human race. Now that the time had come to realize this intention, the divine Spirit found Himself in a human body, an intact one, without experience of the adversary powers; and the divine Spirit now had a pre-vision of how, in this 'sin-free' body, He would bear the sins of the world accruing from the past, the present and the future. Words relating to the 'innocent lamb of God, that takes away the sins of the world' are still used today in the Catholic Mass. He wanted it thus and still wanted it even as He foresaw the immeasurable suffering He would bear. But for this very reason He sweated blood. He foresaw that this whole burden of sin must enter Him, His intact body, *before* the Crucifixion, in order for it to be possible for the unpurified blood to flow out of Him again.

Thus we can gain a sense of the significance of the Stations of the Cross, for this path from sentencing to nailing on the Cross is the step-by-step assumption of humanity's burden of sin. The burden of the wood of the Cross that Christ had to bear, the crossbeams and the upright, were not the only weight on His shoulders. Humanity's sins were the real burden. At every step of the Stations of the Cross they weighed upon Him, and increased with every step; for with every step something entered that had never previously inhabited this body, and which was not innate to it. It had to enter through and during the path to Golgotha, so as to be able to flow out again on the Cross. The sentencing by Pontius Pilate rendered Christ the true Redeemer of humanity from the burden of sin which had driven man out of paradise. Step by step He took one ill after another onto His shoulders, imbuing His pure blood on behalf of humanity with its unpurified luciferic inheritance. He bore this burdened and likewise burdening blood as Cross to Golgotha, where He redeemed it at this same Cross. In unspeakable pain this blood was able to flow out again. It bore everything of a luciferic nature, and its vessel was pierced when He was nailed to the Cross.

When He fell for the seventh time, humanity's luciferic inheritance had found its way fully into Him. It pressed Him to the ground. After this He no longer took up the Cross of humanity's sins. Here let us recall a remark by Rudolf Steiner, which may strike one as a passing comment but is in fact extraordinarily precise: Rudolf Steiner speaks of the exact quantity of luciferic blood that was finally contained in Jesus' pure body, and ran out from it on the Cross through the nail wounds.* This for-mulation once again points to the fact of Christ's

---

* See lecture of 25 March 1907 in *Original Impulses for the Science of the Spirit* (Completion Press 2001).

incarnation, for all spiritual impulses also have to occur in a physical, sensory process and sequence. The authentic integrity and workings of the world of spirit impinge, right into an exact amount of out-flowing blood, on the material world.

As terrible as it may seem, the torments and falls that led to considerable loss of blood fulfilled a higher purpose. During these dire sufferings the Redeemer lost precisely as much of His own, pure blood as luciferic blood was formed in Him during the Stations of the Cross. Thus at the time of the nailing, the same amount of blood was contained in Jesus' body, but part of this had been replaced by the blood He had taken upon Himself as humanity's sins.

This blood which collected on the path to the Cross flowed out again through the nail wounds. And it flowed out by stages, just as it was absorbed in stages through Christ's steps on the path to Golgotha.

Here we witness that cosmic rhythm of small mirrorings of events, with their central focal point in the nailing of the Lord to the Cross. At the moment

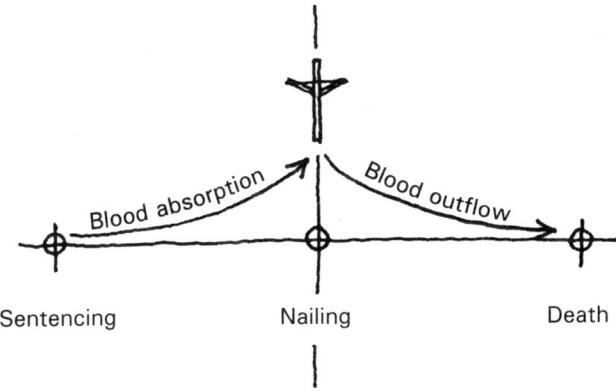

of death, precisely the amount that collected during the Stations of the Cross flowed out again.

As was previously described, the etheric constituents of the pure blood that flowed out during Christ's torture and the falls were gathered together again by the hierarchic beings that descended to earth for this purpose, so as to ensure the pure body would be intact again. This body had to be taken up in its entirety by the earth to fulfil its mission for the earth's planetary body and create the resurrection body.

This is also how we can understand the deeper purpose of Christ drinking the vinegar. Vinegar has highly preservative properties. It was absolutely necessary to impart these natural preservatives to the Lord's body; if He had not drunk the vinegar, something would have occurred that would have rendered the further course of humanity's redemption impossible. At the moment of death, with the seventh word, exactly the amount of luciferic blood flowed out of Him again that had collected in Jesus' body by the time of the seventh fall. At the moment of death the Lord had become utterly human, yet from the same moment the pure Grail blood alone was contained in Him. If, shortly before His death, He had not drunk the vinegar, the pure, divine Grail blood would have burst the physical human body asunder. The physical body could no longer have contained this supersensible blood within it, since, as pure I-bearer, this no longer belonged in the old, physical sheath.

But, for the above reasons, the body should not be damaged by bursting asunder. It was not until the spear wound was given by Cassius that the living blood was liberated intentionally from the 'grave' of the physical corpse of Jesus of Nazareth.

The resurrection body – the first energy form on the path to spirit man

We will now look back to the mysteries of transformation: to the Stations of the Cross and their occult connection with the seven sacred words, and to the transformation of the blood and the formation of the resurrection body as future vessel for this Grail blood. Against this background we can briefly sketch an answer to the question that is often asked about the difference between the resurrection body and spirit man, or atman.*

We have already referred to the special properties of the resurrection body. Rudolf Steiner gained the insight that this new physical form of the human being, which belongs to a future earthly world transformed into etheric substance, continues to possess 'all the attributes'† of the mineral, physical

---

* A future stage of angelic consciousness attained when the physical human being eventually evolves wholly into a spiritual condition. (Editor's note.)
† See lecture of 11 October 1911 in *From Jesus to Christ* (Rudolf Steiner Press 2005).

body. This means for example that — as long as we stand upon the mineral world of earth and are already starting to develop this new body — sensory perceptions are possible *without* the physical sense organs, for this body is not tied to space and time as we generally are in our current physical state. Another phenomenon that can arise through these properties of the resurrection body is so-called bilocation — simultaneous manifestation at different places, a state of being unbound from spatial and temporal earthly conditions. Thus the risen Christ could appear to the disciples and vanish again though the doors were locked. The resurrection form of Christ was also perceived in swift succession at various places, some of which were far distant from each other, without this form having to traverse the distance in the usual way, subject to earthly gravity.

But for what purpose does the human being need this new body healed from the influences of adversary powers. Why does he need to draw it towards him and apparel himself in it, developing from it a seed that is individually suited to him?

This body is (only) *one* step on the path to full spiritualization of the physical body.

Within the evolutionary history of the earth we continually find repetitions of a larger, overarching process in smaller phases: first we have the great evolutionary stages of our planetary body, seven different planetary embodiments. Within each of these larger lifetimes of an earth body, seven epochs succeed one another, each of which is further sub-divided into seven cultural eras. Today we find ourselves in the Earth embodiment in the mineral kingdom and in the fifth epoch, the so-called post-Atlantean. After passing through two succeeding cultural eras, the so-called 'Russian' and the seventh, two further epochs will follow, each of which is subdivided into seven cultural eras. During these future epochs and eras the state of our earthly, physical body will change. We can contribute to this through our physical, soul and spiritual work. When we develop a spiritual view of the world we will succeed in making 'fluid', or 'etherizing', a considerable portion of our degenerating, sclerotic earth, and lead it onwards to the condition it will have at the Jupiter planetary stage. In other words, the planetary body will begin to be spiritualized.

In a corresponding way the human being adapts his own corporeal structure to this spiritualization of the physical world on which he lives. We could equally say that the gradual spiritualization of our physical form also transforms the earth. All these processes depend on the earth being penetrated by the Christ divinity. The Christ being active both in the earth and in the human being can bring us and the earth back to the Father.* Human being and earth once formed out of a soul-warmth condition on Saturn, taking their way into greater and greater density. The Sun incarnation of the earth was already a 'gaseous' one, which passed over into a 'watery' Moon state before reaching its point of deepest density in the mineral realm. Here the Trinity intervened in humanity's course of evolution, as described earlier in this book. On earth, when the Mystery of Golgotha took place, a turning

---

* Of course there is also the extra- or super-cosmic concept of the Father. Here, however, the Father concept relates to the planetary evolution of our earth from Saturn to Vulcan.

point was implanted in us as potential. Through Christ's deed of sacrifice the human being can freely resolve to lead the earth back to the Father. He will — similar to his state on Saturn — again develop a soul-spiritual warmth body on Vulcan, but will at the same time retain, in full autonomy, the I power indwelling him. Thus this return, despite it being to a state similar to the original condition, is in fact a wholly new advance. The human being will become divine, will become spirit man; and the earth will become a sun.

That is the far-distant goal of evolution. The resurrection body is the physical form of the human being that can redeem and transport him from the seventh epoch of the mineral earth incarnation to the Jupiter planetary incarnation. The lowest element of the Jupiter earth will be the mineral earth kingdom spiritualized into etheric. Not until the Venus planetary incarnation will we have trans-formed our body to an extent that we can become spirit man on Vulcan. This will involve complete spiritualization of the body. In a certain sense, Atman corresponds to the physical condition of the human being during the Saturn stage. What there could be called a physical body, though in the greatest possible dilution and non-material state, will have been regained by the human being on Vulcan, transformed into Atman through the incorporating of his I and his work on his lower bodies.

The resurrection body, on the other hand, is *not* the complete transformation of the physical body as this will eventually develop in those far-off conditions, but is rather a kindling, pre-figuring, pre-shimmering of this condition. This is the physical form of manifestation of the human being that is fitted to the new, transformed earth which will lift from the mineral kingdom and spiritualize itself. This is a smaller process that occurs in correspondence to a greater, future occurrence. To our contemporary view the Jupiter condition appears as a 'small Vulcan' and the resurrection body, which liberates the human being from the bonds of material death, appears to us as a 'small Atman'. The resurrection body is the beginning of spiritualization of the human being's physical form.

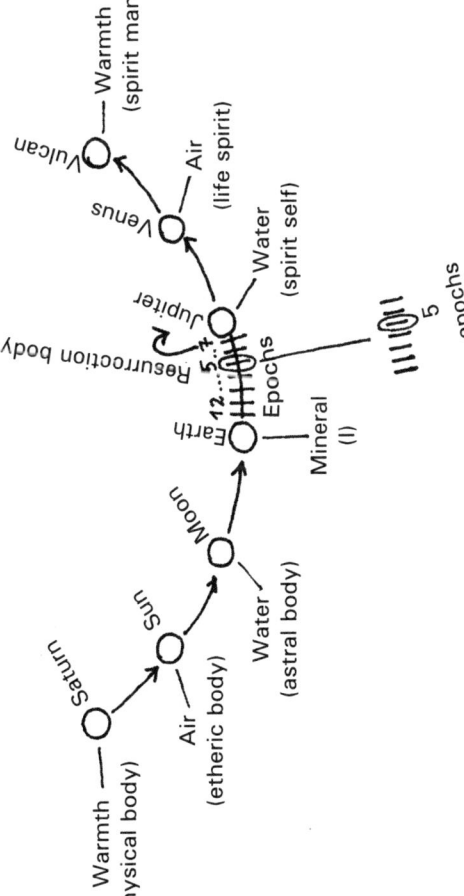

The resurrection body as first step towards spiritualization of corporeality

Thus the mystery of transformation is a new impulse which Christ has implanted in humanity. Christ reverses the descending evolutionary sequence to make it possible for us to attain a divine state. It is now no longer a process of 'becoming' passing into 'dying'. He reverses this to turn 'dying' into 'becoming'. What was once dead acquires life as the human being's physical form is released from the death process.

In reverence and gratitude we honour the mystery of resurrection as recreation of the human being's archetypal physical form. Christ raised this radiant apparel of the future, the indestructible temple of our body, from the abysses of darkness, so that henceforth death can become life:

> *In death eternal life dawned on the soul.*
> *O you are death, and heal us, make us whole!*
>   Novalis*

---

* From the fifth 'Hymn to the Night'. See *Hymns to the Night / Spiritual Songs* (Temple Lodge Publishing 1992).

The Lord's Prayer
The Living Word of God
Judith von Halle

(Approaches to Understanding the Christ Event, Volume 1)

After she received the stigmata in 2004, Judith von Halle began to experience, very vividly, the events that occurred at the time of Christ. These continuing experiences are not visionary or clairvoyant in nature, but an actual participation, involving all human senses, in the events themselves. To complement this method of witnessing Christ's life, von Halle brings to bear a spiritual-scientific mode of observation – a form of research based on a fully conscious crossing of the spiritual threshold by the human 'I' (or self). Combining the results, she describes in this concise study Christ's presentation of the Lord's Prayer – the archetypal prayer of humanity – to those closest to Him, and the context in which He gave it.

Von Halle considers the historical circumstances at the time of Christ, the preparations He made for passing the

Prayer on to others, the Prayer's meaning to the disciples, and how the Prayer itself acts as a mediator between worlds. In addition she reflects on the doxology of the Lord's Prayer, and its relation to the Sephiroth Tree.

96pp; hardback; £9.95; ISBN 978 1902636 85 6